OVERHEAD ESPIONAGE

A Historical Snapshot of US Aerial Reconnaissance

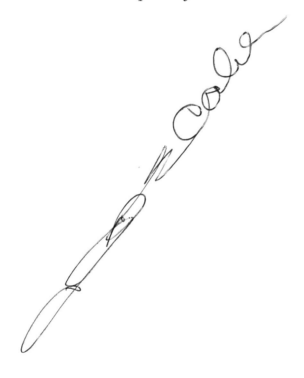

OVERHEAD ESPIONAGE

A Historical Snapshot of US Aerial Reconnaissance

CHARLES E. CABLER
US Air Force Veteran

SUNSTONE PRESS
SANTA FE

Disclaimer:

This book does not represent, promote or endorse NASA, Lockheed Martin, any private company, individual, internet website, or US Government agency referenced within it. This book includes a material research reference to select published data or photographs concerning these entities, but does not vouch for the content or accuracy of information contained within these sites. To the best of the author's knowledge, this book does not contain any classified information.

Sunstone books may be purchased for educational, business, or sales promotional use. For information please write: Special Markets Department, Sunstone Press, P.O. Box 2321, Santa Fe, New Mexico 87504-2321.

Book and cover design › R. Ahl
Printed on acid-free paper

Library of Congress Cataloging-in-Publication Data

Names: Cabler, Charles E., author.
Title: Overhead espionage : a historical snapshot of US aerial reconnaissance / Charles E. Cabler.
Description: Santa Fe, New Mexico : Sunstone Press, [2020]. | Summary: "A historical snapshot of the development and evolution of US aerial reconnaissance as a vital part of our national security and combat support operations"-- Provided by publisher.
Identifiers: LCCN 2021021148 | ISBN 9781632933218 (paperback) | ISBN 1632933217 (paperback)
Subjects: LCSH: Aerial reconnaissance, American--History. | Airplanes, Military--United States--History. | Aerial surveillance--History. | Espionage, American--History. | National security--United States--History.
Classification: LCC UG763 .C34 2020 | DDC 327.1273--dc23
LC record available at https://lccn.loc.gov/2021021148

WWW.SUNSTONEPRESS.COM
SUNSTONE PRESS / POST OFFICE BOX 2321 / SANTA FE, NM 87504-2321 /USA
(505) 988-4418 / FAX (505) 988-1025

This book is dedicated to all members of the US Armed Forces, past, present, and future who proudly serve and protect the freedom we enjoy.

In my view there are two essential elements of responsibility for defending our freedoms, moral fabric and physical strength. The armed forces of the Unites States have provided the physical strength...and...ensure that no foreign government will ever be able to enforce their rule upon our people.
—Colonel Carlyle S. Harris, Ret. USAF, Vietnam POW

CONTENTS

INTRODUCTION

History is filled with information about reconnaissance that fascinate most military history buffs or aviation enthusiast. Aerial reconnaissance, which began as a low-level military priority, has developed into an operational necessity for our national defense. Over the years, reconnaissance work has utilized several methodologies including the hot air balloon, carrier pigeons, planes and now satellites. Each method built on the success, and failure, of its predecessor to create the most comprehensive and effective reconnaissance program in the world. This book relates only a small snapshot of the development of this program, to remember the commitment and dedication of those willing to sacrifice their all to create a successful US reconnaissance program. "Overhead espionage," a descriptive term coined in the early years of aerial surveillance became, and continues to be, a vital part of our national security and combat support operations.

During the early years of WWI (1914–1918), the first use of planes was for reconnaissance purposes using low-level flights with the pilot landing the plane and providing a verbal report. It later involved a primitive effort of map sketching from the air which was, at that time, very useful information to ground units. However, after the suggestion of using cameras to photograph the area in place of map sketching, aerial reconnaissance matured rapidly. Much of this maturity was attributed to the aerial reconnaissance work performed by the countries of England, France, and Germany. The US did not have planes adequate for a strong start in the early years of WWI, but played an important reconnaissance role during the final months flying French made aircraft with modified cameras. After the US entered WWII in 1941, the development and utilization of US reconnaissance aircraft such as the; B-17, B-29, B-130, P-51 Mustang, P-38 lighting, F-4, the U-2, A-12 and the SR-71A increased dramatically.

After WWII ended in 1945, reconnaissance continued to fulfill a variety of US information needs including locations of enemy missile sites, troop movements and activity on military installations.

The Cold War era (1947–1991) created a state of political tension and hostility between the United States (US) and Soviet Union, a/k/a Russia, following World War II. This ideological rivalry involving; propaganda, subversion, espionage, sabotage, threats, economic sanctions, and spying, stopped just short of a full-scale confrontation. It ushered in an era creating a greater need for the US to keep closer tabs on its adversary, the Soviet Union. Unfortunately, the Soviet Union consisted of a vast amount of territory, and keeping a watchful eye became an impossible task for the United States Army Air Corps (USAAC), whose primary mission was to support ground warfare. To accomplish this surveillance objective, the idea for a separate branch of the Armed Forces, the US Air Force, was introduced. This idea was discussed at the highest levels of the government, and struggled to garner sufficient support to become a reality.

General William "Billy" Mitchell, was convinced that air power would revolutionize modern warfare, and achieving aerial combat superiority would be a vital component of a strong US military. Proficiency in aerial combat warfare coupled with the capability of providing aerial surveillance information, would be of great benefit to all branches of the service. However, in General Mitchell's opinion it would require an independent branch of service. With Congressional approval, the National Security Act created the US Air Force (USAF) on 18 September 1947, and it subsequently developed into the world's largest and most technologically advanced air force in the world. As part of its purpose, the USAF was charged to; preserve the peace and security, and provide for the defense, of the United States, the Territories, Commonwealths, and possessions, and any areas occupied by the United States. In addition to developing an aerial combat ready status, a significant part of that purpose included Intelligence, Surveillance and Reconnaissance (ISR). General Mitchell's Air Force became a meaningful part of overhead espionage during the wars in which the US has been engaged, and forty-four years of the Cold War.

The Cold War came to a close when; the last war of Soviet occupation ended in Afghanistan, the Berlin Wall came down in Germany and a series of mostly peaceful revolutions swept the Soviet Bloc states of eastern Europe. First President of the Russian Federation, Boris Yeltsin, in his 25 December 1991 speech acknowledged the Cold War had ended, and on

26 December 1991 the Soviet Union officially dissolved, breaking up into fifteen separate nations. The memories of events transpiring during those Cold War years have diminished over time, and with fewer people from that time period still living, the stories become less available, and often vaguer and more incomplete. For the generations growing up in post-Cold War America, Communism and its consequences are often abstract concepts, existing only within the pages of history books, and with time they become less and less real. Additionally, because of the emphasis on science, technology, engineering and mathematics, history appears to have become less meaningful. According to a survey conducted by the National Assessment of Education, teaching American history lags behind all other subjects taught in our high schools, colleges, and universities. In fact, taking a course in American history is not required to graduate in many US colleges. With less history being taught, and our propensity to forget, it is good to look back and be reminded of the events which established and defined our way of life.

My friend Francis Gary Powers Jr., Founder and Chairman Emeritus of the Cold War Museum in Virginia, tells the story that a few years ago he was invited to speak to a group of high school and college students about the historical U-2 incident involving his dad. When he arrived, and much to his surprise, the students were expecting to hear the history of the U-2 rock group. Gary was stunned that so many students were not knowledgeable of the major US diplomatic crisis which occurred as a result of the U-2 spy plane of Francis Gary Powers being shot down over Russia in 1960.

My conversations with U-2 and SR-71A spy plane pilots and other military personnel who supported those planes, rekindled my interest in aerial reconnaissance. So, I set about to write this book with a focus on a select few notable spy planes, interesting Cold War events and trivia reminiscent of several espionage incidents, and the notable people involved. The book includes personal stories of military people involved in reconnaissance work which I am sure have never been shared with the public. This is not a book recounting hair raising stories of flying these magnificent planes, nor the detailed proficiency with which the missions were carried out. For that type information, I refer you to the many excellent books written by aviation experts I have used and referenced in the research material section. This book is a simply a snapshot of the development and progression of overhead espionage, and great way to be reminded of the men and women, past and present, who so bravely provide the freedom we enjoy in our great country. By no means do I purport to be an expert in aviation or aerial reconnaissance. I am probably not even a good conversationalist on these topics. But as an amateur historian, I am an enthusiast with a deep appreciation for the work many people do in reconnaissance. I hope you enjoy reading this book as much as I did in researching and writing it.

RECONNAISSANCE

Those who do not know the conditions of the mountains and forests, hazardous defiles, and marshes and swamps cannot conduct the march of an army. Those who do not use local guides are unable to obtain the advantages of the ground.

—Sun Tzu, Chinese Military Strategist, 500 B.C.

1

THE GENESIS OF RECONNAISSANCE

The concept of reconnaissance did not begin with a world war, although its development expanded exponentially during war time, making it a military standard operational procedure. In fact, intelligence gathering for military use began so long ago that its genesis is considered legendary.

Evidence of military reconnaissance missions dates back to Biblical time. About 1410 B.C. the Old Testament records that Joshua, the prophet and leader of the Israelite Nation, secretly sent out two spies from the Israelite camp at Acacia Grove with instructions to scout out the land on the other side of the Jordan River, especially around Jericho, in preparation to take the land. Because Joshua was in unfamiliar territory and understood the value of having information about his enemy's position and strength, he needed a reconnaissance mission to prepare for the impending battle. Military strategists tell us there is an acute benefit in accurate information because, over estimating an enemy's capability can be just as great a mistake as underestimating it. With the support and help of a local woman, the Israelite spies completed their mission and returned undetected to report their findings. Using this reconnaissance information, the battle was successful and Jericho was utterly destroyed, due in part to the wisdom of Joshua to seek information about his enemy. In his book, *Operation Overflight*, Captain Francis Gary Powers stated, "The value of intelligence lies not only in knowing what the enemy is doing; often of equal, and sometimes even greater, importance is, they're not knowing that you know."

According to historical authorities, a man by the name of Sun Tzu lived in China in the late sixth century BC was considered by many people to be the ultimate strategist of eastern thought. His philosophic writings have been very influential and have contributed to the development and implementation of eastern military war strategy and tactics. While some believe him to have been a civilian strategist, others believe he was a military general. Irrespective of his position, he is credited as the author of *The Art of War*. In this book, Sun Tzu writes, "Those who do not know the conditions of the mountains and forests, hazardous defiles, and marshes and swamps cannot conduct the march of an army. Those who do not use local guides are unable to obtain the advantages of the ground." Sun Tzu fully understood the principles of, and need for, a reconnaissance mission before undertaking a battle.

Those early beginnings created the process of obtaining information about the position, activities, resources, etc. of an enemy, providing a significant strategic and tactical advantage in planning a battle attack. Military field commanders favor sending small teams possessing the speed, agility and mobility to effectively gather detail information about the enemy, terrain and potential target acquisition before deploying large combat groups into an area. Examples of ground reconnaissance include specialized units such as: US Army Rangers, Special Forces, Special Operations, and Military Intelligence Specialists. Although once used primarily as advance support to conventional combat troop engagements, today special reconnaissance resources have become the new activity front in a complicated world. It has been estimated that at any given time during 2017, approximately 8,000 US reconnaissance and special operations units were deployed around the world.

The first recorded account of aerial surveillance dates back to the 1700s using a French invention, the hot air balloon. The first un-tethered manned flight was made 21 November 1783 using a gondola wicker basket suspended beneath the balloon to carry passengers, and a source of heat to keep the balloon aloft. After the French Revolution (1789–1799) several people were intrigued with the possibility of extended use of aerial reconnaissance, but concerned as to whether or not a hot air balloon could be effective. A noted scientist of the day, Charles Coutelle, was commissioned to conduct studies using the balloon *L'Entreprenant* [translated the Enterprising One] the first military reconnaissance aircraft. As an interesting observation, remember the fictional spacecraft the *USS Enterprise in the Star Trek*® television series? The mission was "to seek out the unknown, to boldly go where no one has gone before...," with similarities to the mission of the French balloon. I suspect there may be a connection to its name.

Balloons became an early instrument of military intelligence gathering and possibly of greater strategic importance, the creation of accurate battlefield maps. However, use of the balloons came to an end in 1799 when Napoleon Bonaparte disbanded the French Balloon Corps. It was not until 1870 that aerial reconnaissance balloons were again employed by the French during the Franco-Prussian War. After the invention of photography, primitive aerial photographs were made of the ground from manned and unmanned balloons, and tethered kites.

We are familiar with the development and use of the submarine during the American Civil War (1861–1865) such as the Confederate *H.L. Hunley* which sank the Union sloop *Housatonic* in 1864. However, a much lesser-known fact is that reconnaissance balloons were used early in the war by the Union Army Balloon Corp., under the command of Chief Aeronaut Thaddeus S. C. Lowe. Master joiners contrived a box containing tanks and copper tubing which when filled with sulfuric acid and iron filings produced hydrogen gas used to inflate these observation balloons. The first balloon, *the Union* was operational 1 October 1861 and although it was a failure, other balloons were successfully used at the engagements of Bull Run, Yorktown, Fair Oaks, and Vicksburg. Using reconnaissance balloon technology during the Civil War seems incredible to me considering combat tactics at that time consisted of mass infantry battle lines and close-range volleys of musket fire. It was a time when armies used European battle strategies of open field cavalry, artillery, and infantry charging at each other. Trench warfare and guerrilla tactics had been tested; however, they were not a prevalent war strategy. Although limited, both the Union and Confederacy used hydrogen filled balloons for reconnaissance.

The first reconnaissance airplanes used during combat missions were by the Italian Air Force during the Italo-Turkish War (1911–1912). On 23 October 1911, Italian pilot, Capt. Carlo Piazza, flew over the Turkish lines in Libya to conduct history's first combat aerial reconnaissance mission. Having an aerial viewpoint of the battlefield and enemy positions proved to be very effective. From this information an interpretation center could decipher details essential to designing a successful battle strategy. Since that first hot air balloon flight in 1783, the need for, and use of, aerial reconnaissance has become a vital part of military strategy and tactics.

As an element within the US Army Signal Corps, the Aeronautical Division, progenitor of the US Air Force, acquired the first powered military aircraft in 1909 for reconnaissance purposes. Since that time, the US Air

Force (USAF) and the Central Intelligence Agency (CIA) have worked jointly to monitor foreign government's military activity through aerial reconnaissance. Their purpose was to collect and provide the National Security Administration (NSA) with photographic evidence of military activity at specific world locations. When the collectors have done their job properly, analysts go to work developing the photographic evidence, analyze it and conclude with a key judgment for making a decision.

As discussed in the book, aerial reconnaissance played a very significant role in the success achieved by the US in the many wars and conflicts in which it has been involved. Aerial reconnaissance came of age during WWII, and throughout the Cold War and extending into today, many important decisions were made as a result of reconnaissance missions. The story of aerial reconnaissance is fascinating as this snapshot reveals.

2

THE COLD WAR

The Cold War means different things to people. For some, the Cold War is just a vague memory with no great significance. For others, it's something they read about in a history book or heard older people occasionally talk about, but it doesn't seem that important today. However, for many of us who lived during that time period, it is a vivid memory. A time of great anxiety, uncertainty beyond imagination, and one we would rather not relive.

Allies and friends who became rivals and enemies brought about the Cold War. The United States and the Union of Soviet Socialist Republics (USSR), commonly known as the Soviet Union, each with a competing view of the world, opposing ideologies, different economic systems, and an arsenal of nuclear-tipped missiles ready to launch, dominated the news as the threat of using a nuclear bomb increased incrementally. Learning to live under the constant threat of a nuclear attack, school children, through regular drills, were instructed on what to do to protect themselves. A cartoon character, "Bert the Turtle", was regularly featured on TV to help teach younger children to "duck and cover." Bomb fall-out shelters were installed in back yards across America, and designated inner-city Civil Defense locations were stockpiled with food, water and supplies. People were nervous about most everything as uncertainty and fear within the US population continued to escalate in this very unstable time.

The Cold War brings back memories of hatred and intolerance of other nations, and skepticism of people who came to the US from those nations. Growing distrust from within and without our own government was so prevalent, it disrupted the governance of our great country and implicated many individuals as being Russian supporters. Fighting to defend his beloved Athens against the invading army of Darius V of Persia in 489 BC, Aeschylus, the Greek tragedian, proclaimed, "In war, truth is the first casualty." Relating that statement to the Cold War, nothing could be truer. A Senator from Wisconsin, Joseph McCarthy, was best known for alleging that large numbers of communist sympathizers and Soviet spies had infiltrated the federal government and were engaged in a conspiracy to undermine the United States.

In 1952 Senator McCarthy became chairman of the Senate's Committee on Government Operations, and for two years focused his time and efforts with his anti-communist investigations and questioning of suspected officials. Senator McCarthy's charges of Russian infiltration led to testimony before the Senate Committee on Foreign Relations to address his perceived problem: disloyal elements within the US government. Apparently, the State Department was one of the most impacted of all governmental groups. Although McCarthy's success has been debated over the years, historian John Earl Haynes concluded that, of 159 people identified on lists used or referenced by McCarthy, evidence was substantial that nine had aided Soviet espionage efforts and could legitimately have been considered security risks. The term "McCarthyism" was coined in 1950 in reference to Senator McCarthy's aggressive attempts to ferret out suspects, frequently in the absence of evidence.

While Senator McCarthy was focusing his attention on government officials, additional investigations were being conducted on US citizens, and much to the surprise of many people, there were communist sympathizers living in the US. Two noted examples were Julius and Ethel Rosenberg from New York, who were spying for the Soviet Union as early as 1940. Julius convinced Ethel's brother, an Army machinist working on the Manhattan Project, to provide him information pertaining to the development of the atomic bomb which he passed along to the Soviets. According to historical records, for the next ten years, Julius and Ethel provided Soviet agents classified information on several US projects including improved radar capabilities and aircraft technology. They were arrested, convicted of espionage and put to death in the electric chair at Sing-Sing prison in 1953 making the first time American citizens were executed for espionage. Many people felt like Julius and Ethel had fallen victim to McCarthy's anti-government environment, but subsequent information confirmed Julius as a Soviet spy and Ethel most likely a spy also.

The Cold War separated loyal US citizens from those who chose to benefit from this opportunity rich environment. Aldrich Ames was the son of a CIA analyst and following his father's footsteps, he joined the agency and had a thirty-one-year career. He eventually became head of the CIA's Soviet counterintelligence division responsible for recruiting Soviet officials into the CIA's spy service. Unfortunately, disillusioned with the spy games between the US and the Soviet Union, and desperate for money, he offered to sell US secrets to the Soviets. Over the next nine years working as a double agent, he received over four million dollars for his information, involving the disclosure of the identities of many American agents working within the Soviet Union. Suspecting Ames as a traitor, the FBI surveilled him for several years, and after finding sufficient evidence of his activities, he was arrested on espionage charges, tried, convicted and sent to prison for life.

Not all Soviet citizens agreed with the communist philosophy or their treatment of people, and while US citizens were busy being traitors, the same was true for the Soviets. In 1977 Soviet electronics engineer Adolf Tolkachev, working in Moscow at the Military Aviation Institute, began a quest to meet with a US diplomat by leaving messages in his automobiles. Although he was ignored, Tolkachev, persisted and eventually gained a diplomat's trust. He began supplying CIA agents classified information which netted him some one million dollars over several years. That proved to be a great investment for the US because information acquired about new Soviet weapon systems, and confirmation that US cruise missiles and bomber planes could fly under Soviet radar, saved the US an estimated two billion dollars in research and development costs. Through Soviet surveillance, Tolkachev was discovered, charged as a spy and executed in 1986.

How did the US digress from a good relationship with the Soviets into a world of hostility, covert activity, distrust, fear and a world in which its own citizens were viewed suspiciously? A quick review of historical events sets the stage for the beginning of the Cold War.

During WW II, the US and the Soviet Union (USSR) were allies with a common objective to defeat Germany, Japan and Italy. Italy surrendered 2 May 1945, just one week prior to Germany's unconditional surrendered in Reims, France, on 7 May 1945 to take effect the following day, ending the European conflict of World War II. Because of the war devastation, Germany was no longer a world power, and posed little threat. The surrender of Imperial Japan was announced on 15 August and formally signed on 2

September 1945, bringing the hostilities of World War II to a close. The US requirement that Japan be completely demilitarized left no concern about them. The Soviet Union had also sustained dramatic losses during the war, and Premier Joseph Stalin looked to his ally for assistance in the rebuilding process. The US attitude of helping other nations prevailed through many years and even President John Kennedy adopted the Woodrow Wilson philosophy that only by making other countries more like the US, would America be safe and secure. In August 1945, General Eisenhower made a visit to the Soviet Union after the surrender of Germany to celebrate victory. During his trip he visited with Joseph Stalin and even watched a victory parade in Red Square. From General Eisenhower's perspective, the trip was a success, and Eisenhower was of the opinion that nothing should prevent the US and the USSR from remaining allies and friends.

However, the ally relationship between the US and the USSR was not destined to continue because these two nations were conflicted based on their ideological philosophies. The US was built on the values of freedom, limited government, and private property ownership. Values worth protecting, as has been done for two hundred and forty-five years. Conversely, in the Soviet Union, Communism was a centralized control government. Its effect would suspend, repress and destroy individual freedom to the extent that freedom could not get in, and millions of people could not get out. One individual visiting the USSR made the observation that after speaking casually with a pedestrian on the street, the pedestrian was dragged away by the secret police. In this type environment, it is no surprise that people spoke in hushed tones, and children did not laugh or play in public as they normally do. Spontaneity was for all intent and purpose nonexistent, and in its place, fear. Freedom of speech, association by choice, open press and religion were events most people avoided.

It was quickly evident that vigorous efforts by the US to advance capitalism and the USSR's promotion of Communist totalism systems in the Soviet Union and abroad could not peacefully coexist. Relations between these rivals intensified, and distrust became a significant watchword in the US government's vocabulary. Both Presidents Franklin Roosevelt and Harry Truman construed Communism to be a challenge to the US capitalistic philosophy and a horrifying alternative for the remainder of the world.

By the end of WW II, the US and the USSR were world superpowers, each active in advancing its respective governmental ideology. Even Adolph

Hitler, the Fuehrer of Germany, recognizing this would be the future, made this statement before committing suicide in 1945, "There will remain in the world only two great powers capable of confronting each other—the United States and Soviet Russia." These differing ideological philosophies prompted another type of war between these superpowers. Not a "hot" war with guns, ships and planes, but a "cold" war of covert activities, sabotage, and espionage to track and stay ahead of what the other was doing. The phrase, "Cold War" was a term created in 1947 by Bernard Mannes Baruch, a US representative to the United Nations Atomic Energy Commission, which adequately described the tense relationship between the US and the Soviet Union which, although very serious, fell short of actual warfare.

During and after WWII, the USSR began an aggressive program to overthrow smaller Asian and European countries and expand the USSR. The United Kingdom Prime Minister Winston Churchill was very concerned about what the Soviets were doing, and more importantly, what they were doing that he, nor the US, knew about. On March 5, 1946, at the request of Westminster College in the small Missouri town of Fulton, the Prime Minister made a speech to a crowd of some 40,000 attendees. In this speech, Churchill incorporated a very descriptive phrase that surprised the United States and Britain, "From Stettin in the Baltic to Trieste in the Adriatic, an iron curtain has descended across the Continent." The term "iron curtain" would be synonymous with the Cold War from that time on. Given the Soviet aggression, there was a significant need to know what was going on behind the Iron Curtain, and the US was determined to answer that question.

In 1950 the State Department and the Department of Defense drafted a report referred to as NSC-68 and presented it to President Harry Truman. This report was the initial framework establishing a formal US Cold War Policy specific to the Soviet Union and its allies. NSC-68 assessed the United States objectives as poorly implemented, calling "present programs and plans... dangerously inadequate." It emphasized the need for covert operations and mandated a significant increase in US intelligence-gathering capabilities. The US would rise to this challenge, but it would be costly. Although NSC-68 did not include specific cost estimates, it called for tripling defense spending to $40 or $50 billion per year from the original $13 billion set for 1950, a proposal which needless to say, met with great resistance. President Truman wanted to curb military spending even after the Soviets became a nuclear power, but rather than outrightly reject the NSC-68 recommendations he instead requested additional information on the estimate of costs involved. However, when North Korean forces crossed the 38th parallel on 25 June 1950, NSC 68 took on new importance. NSC-68 was critical during the Cold War, and would continue to be useful for similar future national security concerns. Dwight Eisenhower, succeeded Truman as president and guided the greatest military buildup and intelligence surveillance in US history at that time, even as cost continued to increase. In his 1961 farewell address he made the statement, "Annually, we spend on military security more than the net income of all US corporations."

That increased military expense was justified for several reasons. Since back in the 1930s, the US was very much aware of the significant Soviet intelligence presence, and that agents were providing Moscow with sensitive US military information even as an Alli during WWII. After the war ended and the Cold War intensified, these agents increased their covert intelligence activities, as did the US. This determination to find out what the Soviets were up to expanded over time, involving several different covert activities which would extend far into the future. Trying to stay one-up on each other, espionage and covert surveillance were at a high point for both the US and the Soviets. Based on information released under the Freedom of Information Act, we know that in 1977 the Soviets were building a new embassy building in Washington, DC. Realizing the unique opportunity, the NSA and FBI simultaneously began covertly constructing a tunnel under the embassy building to increase their ability to eavesdrop. To secure the immediate area and conceal the entrance to the tunnel, the FBI purchased several adjoining properties which they used as observation locations. Unfortunately, this espionage project did not materialize as planned. The tunnel was subject to water leaks, the surveillance equipment did not work properly, and often agents had no idea what room was above them. It could have been a room with xerox equipment, or even a file room. After investing several millions of dollars and fifteen years of non-productive surveillance, in the 1990s the NSA and FBI discontinued their efforts and sealed the tunnel. It was just as well, because in 1989 FBI double agent Robert Hanssen had sold the tunnel information to the Soviets. As would be expected, this espionage effort resulted in public humiliation for the US intelligence community. Hypocritically, during this same time period, the US publicly accused the Soviets of spying on its embassy in Moscow.

In establishing the US intelligence-gathering program, the necessity for aerial reconnaissance was paramount. Consequently, this covert program gave birth to two significant US spy planes, the U-2 and the SR-71A Blackbird. Both planes made major contributions to the defense of the United States and its allies throughout the Cold War and beyond.

The early years of the Cold War also saw the beginning of an arms race between these two superpowers. It has been reported that by the end of 1949, the US had a stockpile of more than 200 warheads and several converted B-29 bombers to deliver them to their target. In November 1952, the US tested the first thermonuclear weapon, the H-bomb, 400 times more powerful than the bomb dropped on Hiroshima in 1945. The Soviets tested a similar bomb six months later. The advanced US nuclear program was an immediate threat for the Soviet Union, and something they had to counterbalance. The USSR became a credible challenge to the US, and remains so today. During President Eisenhower's two terms in office, the US arsenal of warheads increased to more than 40,000 by 1960. Although the Soviets were not as advanced in bomb making, they were also acquiring a substantial stockpile.

President John Kennedy was gravely concerned with the extraordinary growth in nuclear weapons within both the US and Soviet Union. By 1962 the Soviets had developed their own intercontinental ballistic missiles (ICBM) and Nikita Khrushchev, First Secretary of the Communist Party of the Soviet Union, made the assertion that the USSR had 100 ICBMs capable of reaching the United States. Throughout the Cold War, the US and USSR knew each could initiate an all-out nuclear attack with, or without, provocation and needless to say, this realization created an unstable environment in both countries. With this rapid growth of nuclear weapons, it was of great necessity that the US maintain surveillance of its former ally, and other nations. Out of this perilous situation was born the "Overhead Espionage," or aerial reconnaissance program, and a few of the spy planes discussed in this book. These planes were instrumental in conducting spy missions during major events within the Cold War including: the Korean conflict, the Cuban missile crisis, Vietnam, and the Bay of Pigs operation. They performed exemplary services then, and the U-2 continues to provide information today directing our strategic activities in many places throughout the world.

Realistically, the Cold War came to an end with the implosion of the Soviet Union in 1991 affecting some 1.5 billion people who lived under the communist regime. After seventy years of existence, America's Cold War archenemy no longer existed. However, the arms race between the US and the new Russia continued in full force. As the number of nuclear weapons increased and concern for their use grew exponentially, a concerted effort of reforms and treaties, such as the Intermediate-Range Nuclear Forces (INF) treaty signed by the US and Soviet Union, began to reduce nuclear weapons stockpiles. President Ronald Reagan wrote in his diary, "I feel the Soviets are so defense minded, so paranoid about being attacked that … we ought to tell them no one here has any intention of doing anything like that."

With determination and persistence, the US ideology of democracy influenced many nations, and surprisingly the old Soviet Union was one of them. In his resignation speech 25 December 1991, Russian President Mikhail Gorbachev included these comments, "I have overseen the Soviet Union's trip down the road to democracy… We're now living in a new world. An end has been put to the Cold War and the arms race, as well as to the mad militarization of the country, which has crippled our economy, public attitudes, and morals. The threat of nuclear war has been removed… I am positive that sooner or later, someday, our common efforts will bear fruit and our nations will live in a prosperous, democratic society." Those statements were quite a change from the totalitarian Communist philosophy and practice which distinctly separated the US and the USSR during this period of time. Unfortunately, the long-standing Soviet philosophy was not just ideological. It was a cultural way of life, engrained into the Soviet people over many years, and one which would be difficult to change. The succeeding years reflected a heightened increase in mutual distrust between the Soviets and the US.

Conflicts and tensions between the US and Russia remain in existence today. President Gorbachev's dream of living in a democratic society has not yet been realized, and although not as pronounced, the threat of nuclear war with Russia remains. While the exact number of nuclear weapons in each country's arsenal is closely guarded, it is estimated that the US has 6,550 and Russia has 6,800 of the total 14,500 in existence today. The 2010 new Strategic Arms Reduction Treaty (START) signed by President Obama and Russian President Dmitry Medvedev limited each country to 1550 deployed warheads and 700 deployed missiles and bombers. Needless to say, each country continues to engage in espionage to ensure compliance.

The Cold War may have ended, but espionage activity has not. A highly publicized case in 2013 involved Edward Snowden, a former contractor with the National Security Agency. His security clearance permitted him access to a significant amount of top-secret information about the US electronic surveillance programs which he leaked to the public. Although Snowden claims he did this to expose the government's intrusion into the lives of US citizens, the government considered it espionage. It is one of the most notable and egregious occurrences in the history of the NSA. Interestingly, Snowden was granted temporary asylum in Russia.

Henry Kissinger, former US Secretary of State and National Security Advisor under the administrations of Richard Nixon and Gerald Ford, made the observation, "It is not often that nations learn from the past, even rarer that they draw the correct conclusions from it." People continue to be arrested and charged with espionage, and cyber security encroachments today. Therefore, we must consider the old cliché that history repeats itself, and with the possibility of a much more intense Cold War than we experienced previously.

3

OVERHEAD ESPIONAGE, THE EARLY YEARS

When World War I (WWI) began in 1914, the airplane was only eleven years old and its potential uses were still being defined. Consequently, airplanes played only a minor role. However, by the end of the war in 1918 planes had become an important part of the war efforts for both sides. The US did not produce any aircraft of its own design for use in combat during WW I, nor did it recognize the strategic military value of airplanes. Aerial reconnaissance languished as a mission type for the US, and tended to be overshadowed by routine aerial mapping. However, experience would soon prove that bombing efforts were very ineffective without adequate aerial reconnaissance.

As with its predecessor, the hot air balloon, using the airplane for reconnaissance purposes was soon realized and it became the primary means of collecting military intelligence. Although not engaged in reconnaissance at the beginning of the war, the US played an important role during the last months of the war, using French aircraft and modified cameras. In fact, some camera equipment and techniques instrumental for reconnaissance purposes were developed by the US Army Corps of Engineers for civilian surveying and mapping. WW I reconnaissance planes consisted of a pilot and an observer, and predate the use of a camera. The pilot's job was to fly over the area at a low altitude and long enough for the observer to draw sketches of the terrain indicating any enemy locations they spotted. Needless to say, flying low and slow created a dangerous situation. There was no better target for anti-aircraft guns and no easier prey for enemy fighters on the prowl. Once cameras became easier to use, they provided more accurate and detailed information, and eventually replaced the sketch drawings, without objection from the pilot or observer. The camera became a critical war time weapon.

Although the airplane was slowly becoming a viable wartime observation asset, the US Army Air Corp (USAAC) was still reluctant to put any significant emphasis on its utilization. A young man from Milwaukee, Wisconsin named William "Billy" Lendrum Mitchell, watching intently during a 1904 Wright brothers demonstration flight, had become fascinated with airplanes. After graduating Columbia College of George Washington University, he joined the Army Air Corp. and, at his expense, put himself through flying school. Serving in France during WWI, Mitchell attaining the temporary rank of Brigadier General in October 1918, commanding all American air combat units in France as Chief of Air Service. With considerable appreciation for airplanes, he was perplexed and greatly concerned at the USAAC's reluctance to utilize the airplane to its maximum potential. Realizing the air power Germany, Russia, Italy, and Japan had developed, he could not understand why the USAAC's use of the airplane did not extend beyond the basic purposes of mapping and observation. By the end of WWI in November 1918, Gen Mitchell was convinced that only an air force can fight an air force, and openly proclaimed, "The day has passed when armies on the ground or navies on the sea can be the arbiter of a nation's destiny in war. The main power of defense and the power of initiative against an enemy has passed to the air." Needless to say, this proclamation did not set comfortably with the Army or Navy.

Because of his promotion to the permanent rank of Brigadier General of the Army 16 July 1920, he anticipated he would be better received in his quest for a separate air service. He began an open campaign, promoting a separate military branch dedicated to air power. Unfortunately, Gen. Mitchell became too much of a public critic. Through his frustration and unsuccessful efforts to gain support, he chastised government's ineptitude, accusing senior officers of incompetence and treasonable actions of leadership for the failure to consider developing the air service. He openly contended that Army and Navy witnesses in a Congressional hearing intentionally gave false information to deceive Congress, preventing the establishment of an air power service branch. This type criticism did not bode well with the powers that be and in October 1925, Gen. Mitchell was court-martialed, charged with insubordination, and conduct to the prejudice of good order and military discipline. On 17 December 1925, General Mitchell was found guilty on all counts, and sentenced to a reduction in rank and command, and forfeiture of all pay and allowances for five years. Distraught with the verdict and sentence rendered by his peers, Gen. Mitchell resigned his commission 1 February 1926, but not efforts to promote his idea. As late as 1934 Gen. Mitchell was still touring the country, giving lectures on the current state of US air power, and the need for an independent air force.

President Roosevelt eventually became a believer in air power and with public opinion and congress supporting his belief, a change was in the future. In 1935 at the recommendation of two civilian review boards, the next advancement in air service independence began as all flying ground command units were grouped together as an aerial task force under one command, the General Headquarters Air Force. General Mitchell's idea to create an independent US Air Force finally became a reality in 1947, and subsequently developed into the world's largest, strongest, and most formidable air combat force. Andrew J. Bacevich, a retired US Army officer and professor of history at Boston University put it this way in his book, *Breach of Trust*, "The US Air Force defines the gold standard and has done so since the day of its establishment." For certain General Mitchell's 1918 proclamation that the first battles of any future war will be air battles was recalled by many military officers when the Japanese attacked Pearl Harbor on 7 December 1941 and their aerial bombardment destroyed a good part of the Naval fleet at Clark Field. Given his temperament, General Mitchell may very well have said, "See, didn't I tell you."

Unlike during WWI, when the United States was drawn into WWII in 1941, the use of airplanes for combat was far more advanced. Although its reconnaissance value remained unappreciated by many military leaders when WW II began, by the end of the war aerial intelligence photography became an essential part of military strategy. In contrast, Germany fully understood the military value of aerial reconnaissance. In the spring of 1938 Germany was actively invading and occupying Austria and Czechoslovakia, annexing them into the Third Reich, accomplished in great part to its aerial surveillance work. Commander-in-Chief of the German Army at that time, General Werner von Fritsch, predicted that, "the military organization which has the best reconnaissance unit will win the next war." A prediction which proved true as Brittan and the US were drawn into WWII and developed their own effective reconnaissance programs. Although the Germans had an efficient air reconnaissance and photographic interpretation system, unfortunately, they did not continue to improve it. Learning from German mistakes, the US and Brittan advanced the use of aerial intelligence photography and significantly influenced the outcome of the war. Because of its covert nature, reconnaissance received little recognition commensurate with its important contributions made to the war effort. For security reasons, reconnaissance work was not publicized and therefore the public and much of the military knew very little about this important work. Pilots such as Eddie Rickenbacker with the most victories of any American ace were well known, but there were no publicly recognized reconnaissance heroes.

With a focus on strategic bombing, the USAAC began to place a higher emphasis on reconnaissance, and by D-Day, 6 June 1944, the US 8th and 9th Air Force had developed an immense 325th Reconnaissance Wing. The seven squadrons of the 325th provided routine weather recon, pathfinder-services, radar photography and night missions, as well as special operations in support of inserted intelligence agents. D-Day was the largest photoreconnaissance effort ever recorded in history. The Allied Central Interpretation Unit (ACIU), RAF Medmenham, Buckinghamshire, was the Allied headquarters of photographic intelligence. People stationed there reported that in preparation for D-Day, they received the film for development and printing, and interpreted up to 85,000 images per day. The success of D-Day was attributed in great part to advance reconnaissance work. Planes were undertaking eighty sorties a day over the Normandy coast, and more than 3,200 aerial reconnaissance missions took place prior to the invasion, acquiring photographs of key installations and defenses around the five landing beaches. USAAF Colonel, later promoted to General, George Goddard, a staunch promoter of aerial photography between WWI and WW II, used aerial photographs to replicate models of beaches and their defenses. By doing so, ground combat troops could train in invasion techniques which would help ensure mission success.

However, early overhead espionage did not only consist of balloons and planes. The CIA tried to gain any advantage possible in aerial surveillance, and recent declassified CIA documents reveal its Cold War spy-pigeon program. Historians indicate that messenger pigeons were used as early as 1150 by Genghis Khan to communicate with his military leaders on the battlefield, but their initial use for intelligence gathering began in WWI. Pigeons were very dependable for transporting communications over great distances. Flights as long as 1,100 miles have been recorded, with the average speed of sixty mph over a distance of 600 miles.

Pigeons were used extensively and successfully during WWI. In fact, one homing pigeon was awarded the French Croix de quire, a medal recognizing battlefield bravery, for her heroic service in delivering twelve important messages, despite having been very badly injured. During WWII, the British created a special spy unit, and pigeons became a very significant part of their intelligence gathering process. Pigeons could be air lifted and dropped at a specific ground location. Intel could then be put in a container harnessed to them, and set free to return home with valuable information. In addition to planes, pigeons played a vital part in the invasion of Normandy, 6 June 1944, because radio silence was imposed for fear of German interception.

The British pigeon spy operation was largely shut down at the end of WWII, and the CIA became more active in advancing pigeon spy activities. The CIA recognized the fact that a pigeon can be dropped most anywhere they and still find their way back home even across huge and disorienting distances. The CIA made use of the pigeon's unique homing ability by training them to carry a small camera photographing sensitive sites inside the Soviet Union. They were a good addition for CIA reconnaissance work in the Cold War. The declassified files also reveal the CIA attempted to train ravens to deliver and retrieve small objects from window sills. One raven did deliver a small eavesdropping device to a window sill of a building. Unfortunately, no audible sounds were picked up from the device, but the delivery process was a success. The CIA was also toying with the idea of whether or not migratory birds could be used to determine if the Soviet Union was testing atmospheric chemical weapons. How many missions these pigeons and ravens made, and the measure of success which was achieved is still classified information.

After WWII ended, and the differences between the US and USSR became greater, so did the distrust of each other. Russia was becoming an arch rival of the US, and keeping tabs on its military activity became priority one for the US. Aerial warfare was under the command of the Army Air Corps, and because its primary focus was perfecting the ground war, the ability to conduct effective aerial combat and reconnaissance missions was not given the importance many thought it deserved. Advancement in weapons technology by both the US and the Soviet Union, produced the acknowledgement that the US had no reliable way to conduct aerial surveillance of the Soviets. If the US was to determine the military strength of the Soviet Union on an on-going basis, a new focus on overhead espionage was necessary.

The idea of developing a more effective reconnaissance program had been discussed by lower-level officials of government in Washington, but had found no solid support. Recognizing the limitation for reconnaissance work using existing planes, USAF Col. Richard Leghorn had a dream of a special plane which could operate at a high altitude for extended length of time to take meaningful photographs, but it was just that, a dream. Although he received support from two aviation experts, General Henry Arnold and Brig. General George Goddard, Col. Leghorn didn't seem to generate any sustained interest for his idea at the right levels within this new US Air Force hierarchy. If his dream was to ever become a reality, a newly designed airplane would be required, newly developed fuel for this altitude, and special accommodations for the pilots flying the plane. These seemed like insurmountable odds to overcome. However, Col. Leghorn maintained his dream and in 1953 it became a reality when aeronautical engineer Kelly Johnson began developing the Lockheed CL-282, which became known as the U-2.

After the birth of the US Air Force in 1947, eventually each service branch developed its own aerial reconnaissance and combat units producing many heroes, including: WWI USA Air Service 2nd Lt Pilot Frank Luke, the first pilot to receive the Medal of Honor, WWII USMC Pilot Lt Col. Gregory "Pappy" Boyington, a Medal of Honor and Navy Cross recipient, USAF Col. William A. Campbell of the Tuskegee Airmen, who earned two Distinguished Flying Cross awards, Korean War USAF Pilot and Astronaut Edwin "Buzz" Aldrin, who received the Distinguished Flying Cross, General Daniel "Chappie" James Jr., awarded two Air Force Distinguished Service Medals, top Vietnam War USAF Fighter Ace Col. Charles B. "Chuck" DeBellevue, and Lt. Col. Sharon Preszler, first female active-duty fighter pilot to fly sorties over Iraq, to name just a few.

Each Armed Forces branch had its own need for a reconnaissance program. As discussed in the book Introduction, the Air Force was originally under the Army command and consequently, the Army depended on the Air Force for a substantial amount of reconnaissance work. When the Air Force was formed into a separate service branch, the Army lost some of its accessibility to reconnaissance work. Although primarily a ground fighting service branch, the Army did however develop a reconnaissance program of its own. For example, the Army few the Grumman OV-1, which had a lengthy career as a surveillance aircraft. The 73rd Combat Intelligence Company (Aerial Surveillance), located at Stuttgart Army

Airfield, flew missions on the East German and Czech borders using two variants of the Grumman OV-1, the OV-1D and RV-1D. The OV-1D was equipped with panchromatic and infrared imagery aerial camera systems and Side-Looking Airborne Radar (SLAR) system, while the RV-1D was an Electronic Intelligence (ELINT) surveillance aircraft.

The 7th United States Army Air Reconnaissance Support Company (SAARSCO) at Kaiserslautern, Germany flew Cessna L-19 airplanes from bases operated by the Air Force used in forward air control and observation roles. They also had a mobile unit where they received the photographic film for development, printed, plotted the area covered, and then interpreted the photographs. Realizing the extended use of helicopters, the Army eventually incorporated them into its reconnaissance work. The Taylocraft L-2 Grasshopper was another observation plane widely used by the Army during WWII. Today, the 1st Battalion, 211th Aviation Regiment uses the AH-64 Apache Longbow helicopter to perform aerial reconnaissance and screening operations in within a Combat Aviation Brigade. Along with the capability to perform surveillance work, through the use of aerial firepower, the AH-64 can destroy enemy armored and mechanized vehicles. In 2019 the Army at Fort Benning, Georgia, began assessing the use of drones because of its ability to provide rapidly deployable reconnaissance, surveillance and target acquisition capability to establish situational awareness for locations not easily to observe.

Reconnaissance within the Navy had its origin in the Pacific, as it aggressively pursued the Japanese fleet into its home waters and ultimately destroyed it. This victory was achieved in great part through the assistance of the naval reconnaissance team's intelligence. Naval reconnaissance was scaled back after the defeat of Japan, but was not deactivated altogether. Naval aviation patrols continued to support the fleet with aerial reconnaissance to the end of the Cold War. Planes such as the; PB4Y Privateer, P4M-1Q, EA-3B, EP-38, P2V Neptune, P4M-1Q, A3D-1Q Skywarrior, and EC-121 played an important role in aerial surveillance during these years. In today's environment, reconnaissance surveillance continues to provide the Navy with the unique ability in responding and attack planning. Using the intelligence obtained through these reconnaissance missions creates the tactical flexibility to rapidly relocate a launch platform to a needed area. For sea-launched Unmanned Air Vehicles (UAV).

The Marines also have a very active reconnaissance program. The Marine aviation program is divided into six functional units; antiair warfare, offensive air support, assault support, electronic warfare, air reconnaissance, and control of aircraft and missiles. Within these six units, air reconnaissance is considered essential in combat strategy. Through both manned and unmanned reconnaissance assets, aerial intelligence collects information about the terrain, weather, hydrography, and threat situation, and target acquisition. It aids the air and ground operational planning process in mission support requirements to achieve maximum effectiveness through appropriate troop and equipment deployment on the battle field.

Although the reconnaissance program within each of the branches is interesting, the Air Force has been more active on an ongoing basis and therefore the information in his book is more focused on the development of reconnaissance planes and programs within the Air Force.

In the aftermath of WWII, the US faced new world-wide intelligence challenges it had never faced before, and reconnaissance work continued to be carried out by individual military branches. As the demand for reconnaissance information increased, it became evident that a more structured approach was needed to coordinate and control the reconnaissance efforts. President Dwight Eisenhower, recalling the problems of uncoordinated intelligence preceding the bombing of Pearl Harbor, took the position that addressing reconnaissance from a national perspective would create an advantage for the US. Therefore, in August 1960, with the President's support, the National Reconnaissance Office (NRO) was established as a member of the US Intelligence Community, and an agency of the Department of Defense. The mission of the NRO was initially unacknowledged and it operated covertly until October 1973 when a Senate committee report inadvertently disclosed its existence. The NRO was formally declassified on 18 September 1992 as recommended by the CIA Director. The NRO works closely with its intelligence and space partners, and continues to be a significant part of our National Security program as it develops technologies that challenges the expectations of our adversaries.

4

PLANES USED IN US RECONNAISSANCE

Throughout the years, many plane types were modified to fly reconnaissance missions. The B-17 Flying Fortress, B-24 Liberator, and the B-29 Superfortress were just a few modified bombers successfully used during WWII. During the 1950s and 1960s most of the photo and Electronic Intelligence (ELINT) surveillance missions were flown by converted transport aircraft such as the C-97, T-29, CT-29A, and C-130. These aircraft were selected because their size could accommodate the reconnaissance equipment, and hopefully this size plane would not be associated with reconnaissance missions. Unfortunately, their mission concealment was not a complete success, but their electronic surveillance and photography capability proved to be very useful.

The C-97 operated by the CIA, an ELINT gathering aircraft primarily dedicated to monitor Russian air defense radar systems, was successful in gathering information on the SA-2 surface-to-air missile systems which threatened US planes flying over North Vietnam. The C-130 flew most of the photo and ELINT missions during the 1970s and 1980s, and often these flights were designed to trigger Russian defense systems so they could determine the event sequence used to activate the system. US Analyst could then use that data to determine the best way to neutralize the site.

While these modified planes proved to be valuable for higher altitude photography, they were big, difficult to maneuver quickly, and limited in close up photography work. The military attitude and budget did not advocate for new aerial reconnaissance technology and consequently many air crews paid the ultimate price when assigned to missions in lumbering, propeller driven planes more vulnerable to Soviet attacks. When jet fighters were introduced, their usefulness in reconnaissance work was quickly recognized and put to use. However, although these faster jet planes designed for combat use were an improvement over the bombers, they lacked the ability to fly at altitudes beyond the Soviets air defense systems. It is estimated that between 1950 and 1970, over 250 airmen were shot down flying reconnaissance missions over the Soviet border. Some were killed, some were captured by the Soviets, and others were MIA.

As the need for aerial military intelligence continued to increase, it was evident that time was of the essence to develop a spy plane which could fly high enough to avoid Soviet radar detection or at best, Soviet interception. Col. Richard Leghorn, working under the supervision of Col. Bernard Schriever, one of the Air Force's top planners, was assigned the responsibility to assess future US intelligence and reconnaissance needs. Realizing the number of reconnaissance planes being lost gave him and his team more of an incentive to conduct a thorough study as quickly as possible. In his report summary, Col. Leghorn advised Col. Schriever that the US had reached the point when the need to know the capabilities, activities and dispositions of any hostile nation was imperative. As Chief of Intelligence and Reconnaissance Systems Development, Col. Leghorn understood that level of information was available only through aerial reconnaissance. Scientist in the Beacon Hill Study Group endorsed his report and he was hopeful it would be well received by the Air Force and the Department of Defense. Existing aircraft continued to be modified and used for aerial reconnaissance and Col. Leghorn's push for a special spy plane was incessant. Little did he know that in less than two years after his report was published, his research would result in the approval to build the U-2 spy plane.

Several of the traditional combat designed bombers, transport and jet planes used in reconnaissance work are included on the following pages. While there were many other planes which served the US well and could be included, I selected these because many were first type military planes used in reconnaissance work, and considered very instrumental as the overhead espionage program continued to develop.

1908 Observation Balloon, the First Aerial Reconnaissance Device. (Wikipedia Public Domain)

The observation balloon was the first aerial device used as a platform for gathering intelligence and reconnaissance purposes. Balloons were first used by the French in the French Revolutionary War in the 1700s, with the first recorded un-tethered manned flight on 21 November 1783, reaching some 500 feet into the sky. Balloons were also used in the US Civil War (1861-1865) by both the Union and Confederate armies. Little known at that time, but this aerial surveillance discovery would have far reaching use and results.

The first balloons were covered in a silk type fabric and filled with very flammable hydrogen gas, resulting in the destruction of many balloons, their occupants parachuting to safety. Helium, a non-flammable gas, was eventually recognized as a good substituted for the hydrogen gas. One significant factor in using a balloon, is its ability to remain in the sky for extended periods of time. A balloon doesn't require refueling like an aircraft, and therefore is able to provide a continuing source of intelligence as long as needed. As improvements were made, surveillance balloons were able to reach remarkable heights. On 27 May 1931, Auquste Piccard and Paul Kipfer were the first to reach the lower reaches of the stratosphere (30,000 feet) in a balloon.

Initially, balloons provided an accurate view of the terrain for making battlefield maps, a welcome addition in the strategic battle planning process.

If the balloon never filled an additional purpose, the accuracy of maps would have been well worth its development. As the use of field artillery improved gaining the capability of hitting targets well beyond a ground-based observer's visual range, the balloon became even more important. Using an artillery observer in a balloon provided the opportunity to see long-range targets, and give information to the artillery units to adjust the range factors for greater accuracy.

WWI was the high point of balloon utilization. At the beginning of WWI, the Aviation Section of the US Signal Corp. American Expeditionary Force organized its balloon units into company's, wings, and squadrons, and by the end of the war, 110 companies had been formed. During WWII, balloons played a major role in the Normandy invasion. Thousands of Barrage balloons were deployed to Normandy to help defend the already secured beach areas. Barrage balloons were hot air balloons which carried ground connected cables as they became airborne. The balloons would hover at 2,000-3,000 feet above the ground, and if an enemy aircraft hit one of these cables, it would cause significant plane damage. This innovative tactic prevented low level bombing.

After the end of WW II under a project called Moby Dick, the Air Force again began to develop hundreds of high-altitude balloons for aerial espionage over the Soviet Union. These balloons, launched from Western Europe, followed the West to East weather jet streams, and drifted over Soviet air space headed in the direction of US bases in Japan for a mid-air retrieval. The balloons were designed to fly-drift during the day at an altitude of 50,000 feet, well out of reach of Soviet air defenses.

When the balloon returned to friendly air space, the camera box would be electronically released from the balloon and small parachutes would deploy as it drifted back to the ground. The pilot of a specially designed plane would fly close as possible to the parachute, and an extended grappling hook would snatch the box and pull it into the plane. Should the pilot be unable to retrieve the box, it would fall to the ground. A multi-lingual notice on the box provided return instructions to anyone finding the box, along with the promise of a reward for the return. The Soviets soon realized the balloons flew at a much lower altitude after sundown, and began to destroy them. After discovering the purpose of the balloons, the Soviets issued a formal protest to the US for the invasion of Soviet air space, and project Moby Dick was discontinued.

Of the 500 balloons launched during its short term from 10 January until 6 February 1956, only forty-four were recovered. However, these balloons successfully provided over 13,000 photographs covering over a million square miles of Soviet territory, and the discovery of the Dodonovo nuclear facility in Siberia.

And so began the US reconnaissance program using the aircraft.

Wright Model A, First US Aerial Reconnaissance Plane. (Wikimedia Commons-Public domain)

The hot air balloon had been successfully used by the US as an aerial observation and reconnaissance vehicle since the Civil War, and the high point for its military use was during WWI. Wilbur and Orville Wright had invented the first powered aircraft, and made four brief flights at Kitty Hawk in 1903. Based on the success of those flights, the Wright brothers built seven Wright Model As in their bicycle shop during the period 1906–1907. In 1908 the US Army Air Corp. became interested in the airplane as a possible replacement for the hot air balloon, and commissioned the Wright brothers to build a plane. The Army specifications for the plane included a load capability of 350 pounds, a speed of 40 miles per hour, and a flying distance of at least 125 miles. The Wright Brothers built the "Military Flyer," a one-of-a-kind model, with wings shortened by two feet, using the same engine from the Wright model A. The result was a plane of a smaller size from the Model A, with a greater speed.

Liking what they saw, the Aeronautical Division of the US Army Signal Corps., purchased the first powered military plane in 1909 for $25,000 (equivalent to $711,389 in 2019) to be used as a reconnaissance aircraft. The plane weighed 740 pounds with a thirty-five-horsepower engine pushing the speed to forty-two mph. The Army accepted the Wright A Military Flyer on 2 August 1909 designating it Signal Corps (S.C.) No.1. The photo above shows 1st Lt. Frank Lahm and Orville Wright in the first US Army airplane, S.C. No. 1, 27 July 1909.

Five additional planes were placed on order. Two planes were received at Fort Sam on 20 April 1911, a Curtis Model D type IV military plane, designated as Signal Corps No. 2, and a new Wright Model B, designated S.C. No. 3. Both planes were equipped with wheels rather than skids as the original Wright Model A.

The Aeronautical Division created special schools to train its aviators, and developed pilot qualifications. After adding twenty-nine aircraft to its inventory, in April 1911 the first permanent aviation unit in American history was formed and named 1st Aero Squadron.

B-17 Flying Fortress, the First Bomber Used in Combat Aerial Reconnaissance.
(Courtesy United States Government)

The B-17 was a four-engine heavy bomber developed by Boeing in the 1930s for the United States Army Air Corp. (USAAC). It was one of the first bomber aircraft used in combat aerial reconnaissance and mapping. The F-9 was the photographic reconnaissance variant of the B-17. The "F" designation we recognize today is for fighter planes such as the F-16 Fighting Falcon and F-18 Super Hornet. That was not so during World War I. The "F" designation was used for all photographic reconnaissance planes. The letter was used because it was available and, as some people speculate, possibly because "foto" was shorthand for "photo." Because of its service ceiling of 25,000 to 35,000 feet putting it above the German antiaircraft guns, it was considered ideal for reconnaissance missions. However, flying conditions could be miserable. Because it was not pressurized or heated, oxygen masks often clogged with ice and exposed skin could freeze in a matter of minutes. But, the B-17 was a tough airplane. It was able to fly even with the loss of two or three engines. The B-17 had excellent flight characteristics and was well regarded by those who flew it. Rendered obsolete by the larger and more powerful B-29, the B-17 served on after the war in small numbers as a search-and-rescue aircraft modified to drop life rafts by parachute.

B-29 Superfortress, the First Reconnaissance Mission Over Tokyo, Japan.
(Courtesy US Air Force)

The B-29 Superfortress, successor to the B-17 Flying Fortress, was a four-engine propeller-driven, high-altitude heavy bomber built by the Boeing company. Its maiden flight was 21 September 1942, and was flown during WWII and the Korean War. Although designed as a bomber, it was used as an aerial weather reconnaissance plane by the USAAF, and routine reconnaissance for bombing missions over Japan. In addition to weather reconnaissance, it also conducted atmospheric sampling for radiation debris. Each B-29 was fitted with air sampling scoops, called "bug catchers." Particles in the air were collected as the air passed through special filters, and analyzed for radioactive debris after the flight.

With the ineffective Tokyo raid by General Jimmy Doolittle's modified B-25s launched from the carrier USS Hornet on 18 April 1942, the focus increased for a major attack on Japan. The B-29 seemed to be the most logical choice for this attack. The B-29, one of the largest aircraft used in World War II, had state-of-the art technology including a fully pressurized cabin. It had an operational range of 3,250 nautical miles and was capable of dropping bombs at altitudes at or above 30,000 feet, well beyond the reach of the Japanese anti-aircraft guns and fighter planes. By the end of 1943, the B-29 was transferred to operate out of the Pacific Theater.

The 3rd Photo Reconnaissance Squadron (PRS) had been activated 10 June 1941 at Maxwell Field, Montgomery, Alabama, and was very proficient in reconnaissance, flying the photographic reconnaissance version of the B-29, the F-13. After consideration, the 3rd PRS was selected for the Japan reconnaissance missions, and relocated from Smoky Hills Army Air Field, now Shilling AFB, to Isley Field, Saipan on 18 September 1944. PRS crewmembers of the B-29 (F-13) "Tokyo Rose" flew the first reconnaissance mission over Tokyo on 1 November 1944. This was a very significant event because it was the first US plane to fly over the city since General Doolittle's raid some two year earlier in April 1942. A total of eighteen photographic reconnaissance missions were flown out of Saipan by the 3rd PRS prior to the bombing raids against Japan. Intelligence from these reconnaissance missions revealed that over fifty percent of Tokyo's war production industry was spread out among residential and commercial neighborhoods. Bombing these factories would result in multiple civilian casualties and non-military collateral damage, but that could not be avoided. Reconnaissance photo assessments conducted after several small raids confirmed the effectiveness of incendiary bombs to wood-and-paper buildings.

During recent months, several problems had been encountered failing to hit the target with conventional bombs, and an alternative method of bombing was needed. Major-General Curtis Lemay, Commander of the Twenty-First Bomber Command, in an operation named "Operation Meetinghouse," ordered a bomber run to be made on Tokyo at night, at low altitude and deliver a mixture of high explosive and incendiary bombs. The objective was to turn the factories, wooden homes and buildings into raging infernos. On the night of 10 March 1945, the USAAF conducted a devastating firebombing raid on the city of Tokyo by 279 B-29 heavy bombers. Reconnaissance indicated that more than 90,000 to 100,000 Japanese, mostly civilians, were killed and one million left homeless in the most destructive single air attack of WWII. The Japanese air defenses proved to be no challenge with only fourteen US aircraft and 96 airmen lost. According to historians, in initiating the Tokyo raid General LeMay said, "The US had finally stopped swatting at flies and gone after the manure pile."

The successful firebombing of Tokyo proved the US had the ability to penetrate enemy homeland airspace, and project "Operation Downfall," a plan for the invasion of Japan, was put in full development mode. As part of that major plan, supervised by Major General Leslie R Groves Jr. of the US Corp of Engineers, the Manhattan Project scientist at the Los Alamos laboratory in Albuquerque, New Mexico, designed and built the first atomic bombs.

General Lemay found it awkward to maintain the close contact and coordination he desired with the 3rd PRS squadron continuing to operate from Saipan. He gave instructions to move the squadron to his base of operations at Harmon Field, Guam, and on 11 January 1945 the squadron was once again relocated. Between November 1944 and August 1945, the 3rd PRS flew numerous reconnaissance missions over Hiroshima and Nagasaki photographing all primary selected targets. After each mission, the film was processed by the 35th Photographic Technical Unit creating a mosaic view of the entire area. With targets defined, planes ready and crews trained, the USAF was ready to deliver the Atomic bomb.

The USAF flew over Japan, dropping leaflets giving one last opportunity to surrender, advising of total destruction which awaited Japanese cities. Unfortunately, the Japanese government refused to surrender. With that rejection, the decision was made to use the atomic bomb. Although these were differing opinions about whether or not to drop the bombs, consideration for the loss of US life was mounting significantly. One and one-quarter million US service members were killed or wounded in WWII, and approximately one million of those occurred between June 1944 and June 1945. It was time to end this long and costly war.

Flying two B-29 bombers, the United States detonated two nuclear weapons over the Japanese cities of Hiroshima and Nagasaki in August 1945, resulting total devastation. The missions were successful in great part because of the photography provided by the 3rd Photo Reconnaissance Squadron which flew 466 solo missions during WWII. Their legacy continues today at Andersen AFB, Guam, which houses Detachment 1, 69th Reconnaissance Group, flying the Northrop Grumman RQ-4 Global Hawk discussed in Chapter 35.

A total of 3,970 B-29s were built and remained in service in various roles throughout the 1950s. It was retired in the early 1960s.

B-47 Stratojet, First Swept-Wing Turbojet Reconnaissance Bomber.
(Courtesy US Air Force)

During 1947, Boeing developed the B-47 Stratojet, a six engine, turbojet-powered long-range nuclear bomber capable of reaching targets within the Soviet Union. Its origination can be traced back to 1943 when the United States Army Air Forces (USAAF) expressed a desire for a reconnaissance bomber utilizing the newly developed jet propulsion system. It was the first plane to utilize the concept of placing the engines in pods suspended under the wings. The B-47 had a top speed of 607 mph, a flight ceiling of 40,500 feet and a range of 4,990 miles. During its service time, the B-47 set several speed and distance records. For example, in 1949 a B-47 flew across the United States in under four hours at an average 608 mph. The B-47 was operational in 1951, and became the foundation of the Air Force's newly created Strategic Air Command, adapted for several specialized functions. In addition to functioning as a strategic bomber, it was utilized extensively as a photographic reconnaissance, electronic intelligence, and weather reconnaissance aircraft. Driven by tensions of the Cold War, over 2,000 B-47s were manufactured to meet the Air Force demands, and remained in service as a reconnaissance aircraft until 1969.

To counter the B-47s performance ability, the Soviet Union's major priority was to produce a long-range, strategic bomber capable of delivering an atomic weapon. In 1951, Major General of Engineering and aircraft designer, Vladimir Myasishchev, began developing the Myasishchev M-4 bomber, The M-4 was a swep wing aircraft powered initially by four Mikulin AM-3A engines producing a maximum speed of 588 mph, a range of 3,500 miles, and a service ceiling of 36,000 ft. The M-4 was eventually designated as "Bison-A" by NATO.

On Soviet Aviation Day, May 1955, western powers were astonished as they watched twenty-eight Bison M-4 jet bombers fly over. This came as a total surprise to the US which, despite its reconnaissance work, did not known the Soviets had built a long-range jet bomber. Based on assumptions and calculations, CIA information analyst anticipated that if the bomber was in mass production, the Soviets would have 800 planes by 1960. This speculation created a monumental concern of a "bomber gap" between the US and the Soviets which had be addressed immediately. As someone once said, emotions are the filters through which facts often become blurred, and perceived risk is amplified. The envisioned bomber gap created sufficient concern from a military and political basis that it prompted an increase in the budget for defense spending.

Was there a bomber gap? It certainly appeared possible. Although many short-range spy missions had been flown over the the Soviet Union borders, its interior was virtually uncharted territory. The US desperately needed a high-flying, long-range spy plane to help answer this bomber gap question and several more. President Dwight Eisenhower, somewhat skeptical of the alleged bomber gap, and with no evidence to disprove it, agreed to the development of the U-2 spy plane to find out for certain.

To be discovered the following year, this aerial demonstration was just another Soviet Cold War hoax to deceive the US. In fact, only ten Bison bombers flew on the Soviet Aviation Day in 1955. Once out of view, the planes quickly turned around, regrouped, added eight additional planes, and flew past the review stand again. That maneuver gave the impression there were twenty-eight aircraft ready for use, with more on the production line. However, the soon to-be-developed developed U-2 spy plane exposed the reality of the M-4 Bison project.

In 1956 a U-2 flown by CIA pilot Martin Knutson photographed the entire fleet of thirty Myasishchev M-4 Bison bombers on the ramp at an airfield southwest of Leningrad. Subsequent U-2 missions over the next year verified there were no additional M-4 Bison bombers at any other airbases, and provided evidence the Soviet military activity level was very limited. The U-2 exposed this Soviet sham and debunked the "bomber gap" hoax.

C-130 Hercules, First 53rd Air Weather Service Squadron Reconnaissance Plane.
(Courtesy Defense Imagery)

The C-130 is a four-engine turboprop plane built by Lockheed Martin, that began its service time in 1956. Originally, it was designed as a military cargo transport with the unique capability to take off and land on unprepared landing strips. It has been used as a gunship, a search and rescue plane, for aerial refueling, tactical airlift and reconnaissance work. It became the fifth plane to achieve fifty years of continuous service for the US Air Force.

Specially modified C-130s flew a significant number of the photo and intelligence reconnaissance missions during the 1970s and 1980s. Because of the plane's size, it could easily accommodate all the reconnaissance cameras and supporting equipment. With its side looking airborne radar system, it was instrumental in collecting valuable data on Soviet's SAMs during the mid-1960s. Although the C-130 cannot be air refueled, with its standard fuel tanks, augmented by special wing-mounted auxiliary fuel tanks, it has the capability to fly almost eighteen hours at its maximum cruising speed of 300 mph, covering over 3,500 miles. This fact alone made it ideal as a reconnaissance plane.

Weather is always a factor for any successful mission, and prior to the US declaring war on the Axis Powers of Germany, Italy and Japan in 1941, discussions had already begun at Army Air Force headquarters concerning organizing weather reconnaissance squadrons. As a result of those discussions, the Army Air Force Weather Reconnaissance Squadron Number One was formed in August 1942. The new squadron was to operate from Wright Field, now known as Wright-Patterson Air Force Base. Using the A-28 Hudson, RB-17E Flying Fortress, and TB-25D Mitchell and a usual crew of a pilot, co-pilot, navigator, weather officer, radio operator and flight engineer, these weather reconnaissance planes flew ahead of a planned aircraft flight route. Their purpose was to scout the weather and report the information via Morse Code. At the conclusion of the flight, the weather officer sent a report confirming the type of aircraft which could fly safely in the weather conditions. These scouting transmissions and reports were essential information, and therefore were encrypted before being transmitted knowing the Germans could possibly intercept them.

Today, the 53rd Weather Reconnaissance Squadron is the only operational unit in the world flying weather reconnaissance on a routine basis. It was activated in 1944 during WWII as the 3rd Weather Reconnaissance Squadron, with a primary mission to track the weather in the North Atlantic between North America and Europe. Interestingly, the 403rd Air Force Wing information fact sheet says the 53rd began as a bar room dare between two Army Air Corps pilots challenging each other to fly through a hurricane. On 27 July 1943, Major Joe Duckworth accepted the challenge and flew a propeller-driven, single engine AT-6 "Texan" trainer into the eye of a hurricane not once, but twice. One flight was accompanied by a navigator and another with a weather officer. These flights were considered the first attempts to fly into the eye of a hurricane to obtain data and plot its position and direction. Major Duckworth won the challenge and because of his "pioneering spirit," he helped to develop a process which remains a vital part of weather forecasting today. In 1965, the 53rd became the first Air Weather Service Squadron to operate the WC-130.

During the nuclear arms race, 1949 through 1990, the Soviet Union conducted many atmospheric nuclear weapons tests. The US felt it imperative to monitor the impact and results of these tests, so the primary mission was given to the C-130. Existing air sampling equipment was modified and adapted for immediate use, and the Air Force authorized the development of a new C-130B, factory-configured to accommodate the sampling missions. These C-130s became the first weather-mission aircraft assigned to the 55th Weather Reconnaissance Squadron, at McClellan Air Force Base, when the Air Weather Service was given the test monitoring responsibility.

The 53rd Weather Reconnaissance Squadron continues to use the CW-130J aircraft as its weather data collection platform today.

The US jet age arrived in 1945 when the Lockheed company produced the P-38, later renamed the F-80 Shooting Star. This plane was designed by none other than the architect of the air, Clarence "Kelly" Johnson, who is discussed in greater detail in Chapter 7. Understanding America's great need for a jet plane, Kelly submitted his proposed design in mid-June, promising to deliver a prototype within 180 days. His legendary management skills were developing as his Lockheed Skunk Works ® engineers designed, built and delivered the plane in 143 days from the start of the design process. In 1945, the P-80 was the first combat fighter jet to be used by the US Army Air Force (USAAF), with a maximum speed of 594 mph, a flight range of 825 miles and an operating ceiling of 46,800 feet. Although Kelly Johnson delivered the plane in record time, unfortunately because of production delays the Shooting Star saw no actual combat during WWII. The F-80 Shooting Star first saw combat service during the Korean War, and was

P-80A-1-LO Shooting Star, the First Reconnaissance Jet.
(Courtesy US Air Force)

among the first aircraft to be involved in air-to-air combat. During these early years, the military plane designation "P" was for pursuit. Thus, the Shooting Star was designated P-80 from its inception in 1945 until 1948 when the military changed plane designations from "P" to "F" to indicate a fighter.

A prototype per-production model of the RF-80, the YP-80A Shooting Star, was the first jet to be used for reconnaissance work by the USAAF, with two YP-80As assigned to the reconnaissance squadron in Italy in February 1945. To accommodate the reconnaissance work, the nose on the YP-80A was modified to rotate forward and house one vertical camera. A later model re-designated as RF-80A improved the photographic capability by carrying up to four cameras, creating the ability to look forward, sideways, and downward Although the YP-80A had very limited service at the end of WWII, it had extensive service by the 8th Tactical Reconnaissance Squadron during the Korean war, 1950-1953. Overhead espionage had taken its next step in achieving effectiveness. RF-80As assigned to the USAFE operated until 1955, returned to the United States where they remained in second-line service until 1958. The RF-84F

Thunderstreak photo reconnaissance plane was introduced in 1954 as the replacement for the RF-80.

The first nonstop, transcontinental jet flight occurred on 27 January 1946 in a F-80, piloted by Col. William Councill. The flight of some 2,457 miles was completed in four hours, thirteen minutes and twenty-six seconds, at an average speed of 584 mph.

Martin RB-57D Canberra, the First High-Altitude Reconnaissance Aircraft.
(Courtesy US Air Force)

The RB-57D was the first high-altitude reconnaissance aircraft produced precisely for reconnaissance.

It was developed from the Martin B-57 Canberra tactical bomber airframe by the Glenn L. Martin Company in 1953, based on specifications provided by the Air Force. The first US built RB-57A jet-bomber was a licensed version of the British Electric Canberra, and the early-built planes were identical to its British counterpart. Its maiden flight was 20 July 1953. As a jet-bomber, the RB-57 holds the distinction of the first plane to drop bombs during combat.

The RB-57D reconnaissance version originally developed as single-seat aircraft, operated at a maximum altitude was 65,000 feet, making it necessary for the pilot wear a fully pressurized suit. Several plane modifications were required to accommodate its new functionality: "wet wing" fuel cells took the place of all fuselage fuel tanks, and two Pratt & Whitney J57 engines replaced the Wright J65 engines used on all earlier RB-57 models. Because defensive armament and bombing capability was no longer necessary, all armament was removed and reconnaissance avionics equipment was installed in the bomb bay. The wings were enlarged, and to lighten the plane as much as possible, the wings were assembled with a special glue as opposed to the usual metal rivets. This posed a great concern to pilots because many substances could affect the strength and integrity of the glue, including deicing fluid. The surface skin of the wing was only 0.010-inch-thick, and could easily be damaged, even by dropping a small hand tool on it. In Chapter 9, we will see this design technique used in the development of the U-2. The first flight of the RB-57D was 3 November 1955, and the first RB-57Ds delivered to the 4025th Strategic Reconnaissance Squadron, 408th Strategic Reconnaissance Wing in the Strategic Air Command (SAC) in April 1956.

Because only twenty RB-57Ds were built, modified RB-57As were used by the 7499th Support Group at Wiesbaden AB, West Germany in Operation "Heart Throb" for reconnaissance missions over Europe. The 7499th consisted of three support squadrons, the 7405th, 7406th and 7407th, each with a different mission objective and skill set. These squadrons flew routine daily or monthly missions during the 1960s into the designated Berlin airspace, along the East Germany and Czechoslovak borders, and the Mediterranean Sea to survey parts of the Middle East.

Unfortunately, because of poor operational readiness, engine problems, and structural fatigue, the aircraft was retired. On 7 October 1959, RB-57D # 5643 was the first, or among the first, aircraft ever to be shot down by a Chinese Surface-to-Air Missile (SAM).

The F-101 was originally designed and manufactured by the McDonald Aircraft Company for the Strategic Air Command (SAC) with the utilization concept as a long-range bomber escort. However, because of its versatility, it was modified and entered service as a nuclear-armed fighter-bomber and continued as such until 1966 when its removal process began. The first flight was made 29 September 1954, and the first F-101 was delivered 2 May 1957 to the Air Force 27th Strategic Fighter Wing.

F-101A Voodoo, the First Supersonic Photo Reconnaissance Plane.
(Courtesy US Air Force)

During its service life, the F-101 worked as an attack fighter, interceptor, fighter-bomber, and reconnaissance plane in the Air Force Strategic Air Command, Air Defense Command, and Tactical Air Command. A total of 807 F-101s were manufactured for the Air Force.

The USAF, looking for a replacement for the RB-57D Canberra, requested McDonald build two F-101 versions to be used Tactical Reconnaissance planes; a RF-101A photoreconnaissance version, and a RF-101C single-seat reconnaissance version. McDonald responded using the basic F-101 airframe, but removing the radar system and four twenty mm cannons, and reshaping the nose to accommodate up to six cameras. The redesigned RF-101A Voodoo was the first supersonic photographic reconnaissance plane used by the USAF. It's two 15,000-pound-thrust Pratt & Whitney J57-P-13 axial-flow turbojets generated a speed of 1,009 mph, with a working ceiling of 38,900 feet. It set a world speed record of 1,207 mph on 12 December 1957 over the Mojave Desert in California.

In addition to reconnaissance missions flown by the U-2, RF-101A pilots with the 363rd Tactical Reconnaissance Wing, Shaw AFB, South Carolina, flew eighty-two reconnaissance missions over Cuba during the 1962 missile crisis. They flew as low as possible to avoid Soviet surface-to-air missiles hits, and one RF-101 pilot tells a story that he flew so low that a soviet volleyball almost hit his plane. Now, that's low flying. The RF-101A also saw considerable service time in Vietnam. They were active in a reconnaissance role until 1979. The RF-101H and RF-101G were remanufactured versions of the F-101As, and continued service as reconnaissance aircraft with the Air National Guard until 1982 when they were officially retired.

A Cuba reconnaissance photo taken 6 November 1962.
Note the shadow of the F-101 below the long building.
(Courtesy US Air Force)

The B-58 was produced by the Convair firm of Fort Worth, Texas, which merged with the General Dynamics Corporation in 1954. It was developed for SAC during the 1960s as the result of the USAF desire to have a supersonic, long range, bombardment aviation platform. The B-58 was the first operational high-altitude jet bomber originally intended to fly at Mach 2 supersonic speed to avoid Soviet fighters. It was introduced into service and operated by two bomb wings, the 43rd Bombardment Wing and the 305th Bombardment Wing of the SAC. March 1960.

B-58 Hustler, the First Reconnaissance Plane Capable of Flying at Mach 2.
(Courtesy US Air Force)

The B-58 was operated by a crew of three: pilot, bombardier/
navigator, and defensive systems operator seated in separated tandem
cockpits. The B-58 was powered by four General Electric engines, each
producing some 15,000 pounds of thrust in afterburner mode. This plane
was unique in that it could operate at supersonic speeds at a 60,000 feet
ceiling, and fly more than 4,500 miles without refueling. It could also fly
at a near-supersonic speed at 500 feet and avoid radar.

Although not designed for reconnaissance purposes, its uniqueness
made it desirable for some special reconnaissance work. A variation, RB-58A,
was developed in January 1956 equipped with a, still under development,
Hughes AN/APQ-69 special photo reconnaissance pod, that would carry a
side-looking radar set. This technology was eventually perfected and used in
future tactical reconnaissance aircraft. In part because of its ability to fly so
low at near-supersonic speed, a second revision of the B-58A was produced
in 1958 incorporating a terrain mapping system that could be used from
either side, or both sides of the aircraft simultaneously. Because B-58 pilots
were the only USAF pilots experienced in long-duration supersonic flight,
several former crew members were selected to fly the SR-71A Blackbird at
the beginning of that program.

Unfortunately, the B-58 was an expensive aircraft to fly and maintain. It required substantial maintenance and special equipment, which was also expensive. Published information indicates that the average maintenance cost per flying hour for the B-58 was $1,440 compared to $1,025 for the B-52. Or to put it another way, the cost to operate two B-58 wings, of thirty-nine planes per wing, was equal to operating six B-52 wings of only fifteen planes per wing. Additionally, the B-58 suffered a high accident rate. Because of these two factors, the B-58 brief service career lasted only from 1960-1970.

RF-4C Phantom II, the First In-Plane Film Processing and an Ejectable Cassette System.
(Courtesy US Air Force)

Many jet fighters were used in reconnaissance missions, including stripped down versions of the P-51 (F-4) and P-38 (F-5), both excelling in high-resolution photography at low altitudes. But the most notable USAF Tactical Reconnaissance aircraft, was the RF-4 C Phantom II used from 1966-1992. The McDonnell Corporation designed the RF-4C fighter with a nose cone that could be easily converted from a fully armed fighter into three optical cameras equipped plane. According to *Modern Spy Planes*, later advancements permitted the film to be processed during the flight and ejected in a sealed cartridge for pick up by front-line combat personnel. How's that for efficiency?

However, as would be expected, replacing the RF-4C's armament with cameras left it defenseless and vulnerable to ground fire. In a conversation with Technical Sergeant (TSgt) Mark Taylor, USAF Weapons Specialist, 117 Tactical Recon Wing, he told me, "Although the reconnaissance version had no armament, the F-4 always carried a full load of chaff and flare countermeasures in the rear fuselage on each mission. We drilled regularly on 'combat turns' of unloading empty countermeasure cartridges and reloading full cartridges, maintaining a turnaround proficiency rating time of a ten to fifteen minutes. But the most challenging process of all was performing this drill wearing chemical warfare protective clothing. That was never a fun activity."

For optimum photographic coverage, the cameras required the RF-4 to fly a straight flight pattern and level at about 5,000 feet. Unfortunately, this predictable pattern resulted in taking enemy fire on most every mission. With a top speed of over Mach 2.2, the RF-4C relied heavily on its speed and agility as its primary defense.

Former USAF fighter pilot James D. Murphy, who flew the RF-4C, made this comment in his book *Business is Combat,* "As soon as I grabbed the canopy rails and let myself down into the cockpit I thought, this feels right." The RF-4 plane was one of the most versatile in the USAF fleet because its powerful Rolls-Royce Spey engines would permit a quick change to adapt to any mission requirement. Murphy further stated, "I can be flying at Mach 1, 500 feet off the hot desert floor and the next minute I can be rolling over on my back and flying inverted over a 12,000-foot mountain..." At full capacity, the RF-4C had a climb rate of 41,000 feet per minute.

Combat situations are always changing, and a pilot must be able to adapt quickly. The RF-4C was always responsive for a quick change. That's one reason pilots liked it. Because the plane maintained a normal work altitude, pilots had to rely on a fast exit should they be tagged by ground radar or be forced to outrun a ground-to-air missile or an air-to-air missile. With its J79-GE-2 engines, each producing 16,100 lbf (pound-force) of afterburner thrust and a top speed of Mach 2.23, the RF-4C was suited for these reconnaissance missions.

5

RECONNAISSANCE SATELLITES

Corona, the First Reconnaissance Satellite.
(Courtesy NASA)

Satellites have been part of our life and conversation since the Soviet Union launched the first satellite, Sputnik 1, in October 1957. In essence, it was the inaugural satellite of the space age. The US, a little behind the Soviets in development, launched its first satellite, Explorer I, in January 1958. Since that time, satellites have been launched by many nations and used for communications, meteorology, weather, global positioning and surveillance purposes.

The US was very much aware that the Soviets knew about and tracked, the U-2 which began its reconnaissance flights in August 1955. The US also knew that the Soviet's SAM could not reach the 60,000-70,000 feet working altitude of the U-2, but that would probably be a short-lived situation. So, in 1955 the US Air Force started an exploratory satellite design project known as "Discoverer" as part of the satellite reconnaissance and protection program. In 1958 the project was transferred to Advanced Research Projects Agency as a joint venture between the Central Intelligence Agency Directorate of Science and Technology and the Air Force. Both groups wanted control of the program and without a resolution, President Eisenhower created the National Reconnaissance Office (NRO) on August 25, 1960. He staffed the NRO with people from both the CIA and the Air Force and charged it with oversight of all US space surveillance programs. The result of the Discoverer project was the development of Corona, the first US series of reconnaissance satellites.

By 1960 U-2 US intelligence agencies were aware that the Soviets had improved their SAMs and overflights were becoming far riskier. Because of the Soviet's concerted improvement efforts, it was just a matter of time until something happened to the U-2, and so it did. In 1960, the U-2 flown by Gary Powers was shot down over Russia ushering in the need for new options in US surveillance. The Corona with its problems and limitations was the fallback option. Initially, the Corona project was beset with numerous operational, and navigation problems. In addition, the cameras produced photos which were lacking in the clarity and detail needed for an acceptable assessment. Often the photographs contained mysterious border fogging and bright streaks which appeared irregularly on the returned film, a problem which was eventually corrected. Because there was no real time transmission of the photos back to a centralized receiving facility, a reentry canister containing the film separated from the satellite on command and fell to earth. It was intended to be caught in mid-air by a passing plane using a towed airborne claw.

Recovery of Film Canister by a C-119.
(Courtesy NASA)

Despite the initial problems, the Corona was a success providing the much-needed reconnaissance information from June 1959 through May 1972 as an adjunct to the U-2 and SR-71 flights. In fact, President Lyndon Johnson made this statement in 1967. "I wouldn't want to be quoted on this ... We've spent $35 or $40 billion on the space program, and if nothing else had come out of it except the knowledge that we gained from space photography; it would be worth ten times what the whole program has cost. Because tonight we know how many missiles the enemy has and, it turned out, our guesses were way off. We were doing things we didn't need to do. We were building things we didn't need to build. We were harboring fears we didn't need to harbor."

There was also an imposing need to address the reconnaissance program in a more economical way. As previously noted, the utilization of reconnaissance planes was becoming increasingly expensive. The SR-71, the primary spy plane's estimated cost to keep it operational was $100,000 per flying hour. At one point in time, the total operational and maintenance expense for the fleet of thirty-two SR-71s was comparable to the cost of maintaining two tactical fighter wings. Although the SR-71 was very effective, the budget could no longer support this expense and the program was shut down in 1999. Because the older U-2 operated at much less expense, the program was reactivated and remains in use today for special purpose reconnaissance.

Since those early years of Corona, hundreds of reconnaissance satellites have been launched by the US through such programs as: SAMOS (1961-1963), MIDAS (1960-1966), Gambit (1963-1984), Hexagon (1971-1986), using platforms such as the Keyhole series (1962–present day). These satellites perform many critical functions including: early warning detecting a ballistic missile launch, nuclear explosion detection identifying nuclear explosions, photo surveillance imaging specific locations, electronic reconnaissance intercepting radio waves, and radar imaging to obtain terrain and land cover information. A satellite is effective and economical but unfortunately it also has its limitations including the same atmospheric and weather disturbances that affect most imagery systems. In addition, a satellite's schedule is predictable; therefore, it is vulnerable to denial and deception practices and signature control activities, creating the continued need for reconnaissance aircraft.

Although many nations have launched spy satellites, the US and Russia own the most. According to Statista Research as of March 31, 2019, the US owns 901 of the 2,062 active satellites orbiting the Earth.

UNIQUE PLANES DESIGNED
FOR OVERHEAD ESPIONAGE

We are deeply concerned over the lack of adequate intelligence data from behind the Iron Curtain.
> —Former President Herbert Hoover, Chairman, President Truman's 1947 Presidential Commission

6

SPECIALLY DESIGNED SPY PLANES

The USAF and the CIA have monitored military activity of foreign governments through aerial reconnaissance, and helping to fulfill that reconnaissance requirement for forty-four years was the U-2, the A-12 Oxcart, and the crown jewel of spy planes, the SR-71A Blackbird. These planes, developed by the Lockheed Corporation Skunk Works Division® and operated by the Central Intelligence Agency (CIA) and the USAF from 1955 to 1999, would be recognized as agents of change in the covert world of aerial reconnaissance. These Cold War spy planes were cloaked in secrecy from their development throughout their military service. Of these three aircraft, the SR-71A Blackbird was an aircraft with the most advanced flying capability and incredible spying technology. Its innate value was determined by its technological development, aeronautical achievements, unmatched performance records, the courage of the men who flew this spectacular plane, and the dedicated people who kept it flying.

From the first spy plane missions in early 1946 until the CL-282 (U-2) project Aquatone was approved in November 1954, a major political and military battle concerning the need for a reconnaissance program had ensued. President Eisenhower, having a full understanding of the need for the US to have an effective aerial reconnaissance program, once made the statement, "The knowledge which only overhead reconnaissance can provide is absolutely vital for the United States." Eisenhower gave his approval emphasizing he did not want the project to be under US military authority. He expected the CIA to have exclusive direct oversight of the project. With his approval, the US was poised to become the world leader in designing and developing aircraft specifically for reconnaissance purposes. While other nations continued to modify existing aircraft for reconnaissance use, the US understood the long-term benefit of a single use, special purpose plane. Rather than continuing to modify an existing air frame, which restricted the effective use of cameras, the US designed the frame to accommodate a full range of unrestricted camera views.

The first US specially designed spy-plane was the Lockheed CL-282 (U-2). It was effective as a spy plane from 1955 until 1960 when one was shot down over the Soviet Union and a large part of it recovered by the Soviets. The Cold War was in full mode, and a replacement for the U-2 was needed.

The next spy plane was the CIA A-12 Oxcart, used from 1962 to 1968. Unfortunately, the A-12 was complex to fly, overburdened its pilot and sustained many mechanical and flight issues. It had a limited life and served as the prototype for a much more advanced and sophisticated spy plane, the USAF/CIA SR-71A Blackbird. Detailed information about the A-12 is included in Chapter 14.

The SR-71A Blackbird was without a doubt the most effective reconnaissance plane ever used by the US With its splendor, magnificence and effectiveness, it maintained an awesome presence in the air. It has been appropriately referred to as, *the seeker of truth without peer or equal.* A fleet of thirty-two SR-71A Blackbirds flew reconnaissance missions from 1964 until the program was officially closed in December 1999.

The SR-71A program consisted of a very elite group; in fact, Col. Richard H. Graham in his book, *Flying The SR-71A Blackbird,* states the program had only ninety-three operational pilots and eighty-nine operational Reconnaissance System Officers (RSO) during its twenty-five years of service. According to a list posted on the *SR-71A On Line* website, only 478 people have ever flown in the Blackbird. To put that in perspective the website observes that more people have climbed to the top of Mount Everest than have flown in the Blackbird.

Many of the design innovative concepts and the overall success of the U-2, A-12 and the SR-71A is attributed to American aerospace engineer and Lockheed's Vice President and Chief of Advanced Research and Development, Clarence "Kelly" Johnson, introduced in Chapter 7 as "the architect of the sky." Designing each plane proved to be a daunting task for Kelly and his team, but when asked about the complexities developing the Blackbird, Kelly replied, "It was no easy task. Everything about the

SR-71A had to be invented from scratch...the design, the technology, even the materials," and many of the tools used to build the plane as well. To put Kelly's statement in perspective, I like the observation made by the German philosopher Arthur Schopenhauer who said, "Talent hits a target that no one else can hit, but Genius hits a target no one else can see." The Blackbirds became a reality only through the visionary genius of Kelly Johnson. Detailed information about the SR-71A is included in Chapter 19.

7

THE ARCHITECT OF THE AIR

Kelly Johnson (left) and Francis Gary Powers in front of a U-2
(Courtesy US Air Force)

Keeping tabs on Soviet activity was a priority for the US. However, the vast size of the Soviet Union made it difficult to survey because of the flying limitations of existing aircraft. Additionally, the Soviet aggressiveness and development of SAM missiles put any plane in danger of being shot down. The US desperately needed a high-altitude reconnaissance aircraft. The response to that need was a plane developed by aeronautical engineer

Kelly Johnson, who in 1953 began developing the Lockheed CL-282. An aircraft design incorporating the profile of a traditional glider, with long, tapered wings, one third the weight of a normal plane, and capable of flying at altitudes to avoid the Soviet's air-to-ground missiles. The CL-282 (U-2) spy plane was an extraordinary aircraft requiring extraordinary perception, knowledge, talent and aerial design. Someone possessing those qualities who could see in reality what no one else could even imagine. That person was Clarence L. "Kelly" Johnson, often referred to as "the architect of the air."

Kelly demonstrated exceptional intelligence, talent, and ambition at a very young age. His interest in, and understanding of, aviation was evident at age twelve when he submitted his first plane design he called "Merlin" after the wizard in King Arthur's court in a local contest, and won a prize. Kelly knew he wanted to design airplanes when he grew up. If there is any credence in being called to a career, it was manifested in Kelly. His ambitions and accomplishments were in full force until he retired from Lockheed Skunk Works® in 1975, and even then, he remained a Lockheed consultant and a personal advisor to Ben Rich in the Advanced Design Department.

Kelly was another rags-to-riches story. He was born February 27, 1910 in Ishpeming, Michigan to poor parents. His father was a carpenter and bricklayer and his mother often took in washing to help support the family. Kelly, or Clarence as he was known then, helped his mother by delivering the freshly laundered clothing in his wagon. It is said that he was so ashamed of his family's poverty, he traveled the back streets on his delivery to avoid people on the main city thoroughfares. He was determined to overcome his poverty, and he did.

In grade school, Clarence was teased unmercifully about his name by his schoolmates calling him "Clara." Although he tried to slough off their teasing, one day young Clarence became so infuriated he tripped a boy in his class and the boy broke his arm. Subsequent to that incident the teasing stopped and Clarence acquiring the nickname "Kelly" after a popular song of that day. From that time on, Clarence was Kelly to everyone.

After high school, Kelly enrolled in Flint Junior College where he studied physics, mathematics and calculus and then the University of Michigan on a scholarship earning a Bachelors and Masters Degree in Aeronautical Engineering, graduating in 1932. As an aviation enthusiast, he applied for the Army's Air Corps, hoping to become an aviation cadet, but was rejected because of an old eye injury. He was hired by Lockheed in 1933 as a tool designer for eighty-three dollars per month until there was an opening in the engineering department. He was described as creative, dynamic, ambitious, and unafraid to question others' expertise and ideas. Demonstrating his bold and outspoken nature, Kelly recognized several deficiencies with the new model Electra 10 plane, pointed those out to the Electra's chief engineer, and made recommendations for improvements. Kelly's design recommendations were such a success, he was promoted to aeronautical engineer at the age of twenty-three, and his career in aircraft design at Lockheed began. The Electra 10 was the aircraft flown by Amelia Earhart in 1937, and the first aircraft to perform a round trip commercial flight over the Atlantic Ocean thanks to Kelley's design corrections.

Kelly was chief engineer in the development of the three spy planes: The U-2, the A-12 and the SR-71A. After WWII, the US soon realized the Soviet Union would no longer be the ally as it had been during the war years. During the 1950s, the Soviets became more aggressive, creating the necessity for on-going aerial surveillance to determine their capabilities and intentions. In response, the Soviet air defense began attacking any aircraft flying near their border. Because of their size and limited maneuverability, the B-17, B-24, B-29 and the B-52, used for reconnaissance, were vulnerable to Soviet anti-aircraft artillery, missiles, and fighters. The US needed a special spy plane which could fly at an altitude high enough to evade Soviet ground radar, and one the Soviet Union's best interceptor, the Mig-19, could not reach to fire air-to air missiles.

Under the code name "Bald Eagle," the USAF requested design proposals for a new reconnaissance aircraft from: American Bell Aircraft Corporation, the Glenn L. Martin Company, and Fairchild Engine and Airplane Company. When Lockheed learned about the design request, it decided to submit an unsolicited proposal and put Kelly in charge of the project. Kelly was its best aeronautical engineer, and responsible for the success of the P-38, the P-80, and several other planes. Lockheed knew that if they received the contract, Kelly could manage both the design and production of this project. In addition to his superior avionic design knowledge, he was also an astute manager known for completing projects ahead of schedule, and on budget. He developed fourteen operational rules as a way to implement his core principles, and he and his team lived by these rules.

Kelly's design was accepted by the USAF and in March 1955

Lockheed received a $22.5 million-dollar contract for the first 20 aircraft. Lockheed met their agreement by delivering the first aircraft in July 1955, and the last aircraft by November 1956 at $ 3.5 million dollars under budget. The aircraft, originally named CL-282 during its development, was renamed the U-2 in July 1955. Aviation engineers say that the key to the aircraft's longevity is its robust and efficient design. These engineers agree that Kelly Johnson, the man who designed the U-2, "got it right."

The U-2 shootdown involving Gary Powers in 1960 paralyzed the US reconnaissance program, forcing changes in policy, procedures, and security protocol. The United States had to move swiftly to develop another plane if an effective reconnaissance program was to continue. Once again Kelly and his Lockheed Skunk Works® team were called on to design this new spy plane. Under Kelly's vision and oversight the A-12 and the SR-71A were developed. The Blackbird program was so successful many of the design elements, logistics and avionic principles learned from it are still being used today in the USAF's development of hypersonic aircraft.

Kelly Johnson was an American Aerospace Pioneer described by his coworkers as imperious, passionate, and demanding. With a short fuse, he often displayed his temper and threatened firing as a rhetorical approach to a mistake. One engineer said Kelly fired him several times during the course of one day. According to research articles, he was just as likely to deliver a kick in the seat of someone's pants as a compliment to his face.

Kelly died December 22, 1990 at the age of 80, leaving a legacy of designing and creating some forty military and civilian aircraft. Once asked in an interview, what plane in his opinion, was the most important plane ever built, Kelly replied, "The crop-duster," a type of plane he had never previously designed, "because that plane made it possible to feed the world." During his career he received countless medals, recognition and honors including Collier Trophies, the Medal of Freedom, National Medal of Science, and National Security Medal.

He lived by the motto "Be quick, be quiet, be on time." He truly was an architect of the air.

8

THE DRAGON LADY

Lockheed CL-282 (U-2), the First High-Altitude Special Reconnaissance Plane.
(Courtesy US Air Force)

As distrust between the US and the Soviet Union continued to grow, so did the escalation of nuclear bomb development, creating an increasing need for the US to expand air surveillance of the Soviet Union. During the late 1940s and into the early 1950s the demand for military intelligence continued to increase incrementally, and the ability to obtain that intel was not improving in relation to the need. President Eisenhower made a comment in his memoirs to the effect that when compared to the

Soviets, the US position for intelligence could not be worse. Using existing planes appeared to be an effort in futility because of their limitations and there was no consensus on how to gather this intel. More American planes on reconnaissance missions were coming under attack as they flew closer to Soviet airspace, and several were shot down. Despite the fact that Allen Dulles, Director of Central Intelligence, favored human intelligence gathering over technical methods, the Air Force convinced President Eisenhower that the future of reconnaissance was in satellites not planes. Consequently, the Air Force focused their efforts on developing a satellite. Despite the failure of twelve launches, rocket engines which did not operate properly even after a successful launch, and unreliable stabilization systems, the President continued to support that program.

Anticipating the future need, in 1953 the CIA had secretly engaged Lockheed's aeronautical engineer Kelly Johnson to begin the development of a high-altitude spy plane. Finally, in 1954 President Eisenhower, considering the failures of the satellite program and wanting to proactively forestall any Soviet aggression attempt, approved the proposal for a special reconnaissance plane. Lockheed, with a budget of $22 million ($ 207 million in 2019), started project Aquatone, and its engineers went to work.

Despite the increasing demand for intelligence, there were many differing opinions about whether or not a reconnaissance program was really necessary, and if so, was it prudent to fund the development of a special plane given the current budget constraints. How much would the plane cost? Where would the expense be charged? Whose budget would be impacted? All questions without answers. The President preferred the program not be included in the Defense budget, primarily because it would no longer be the secret program it needed to remain. On a temporary basis, funding the CL-282 through the CIA covert activity contingency fund seemed to be the easiest and quickest way to get the project underway and still maintain its secrecy. The president knew full well that the CL-282 could not be funded through the CIA covert activity contingency fund indefinitely. At some point in time, it would need funding through the general budget. He also knew the cost of maintaining the CL-282 program would carry several negative project resistance and economic impacts to the US budget in future years. That, however, could not be the determining factor in whether or not to keep the program operational to monitor the Soviet military activity. To help mitigate these negative impacts but remain knowledgeable of Soviet nuclear strength, President Eisenhower, proposed the "Open Skies" policy to the representatives of France, Great Britain, and the Soviet Union at the 1955 Geneva summit. This policy would have created a mutual East-West aerial reconnaissance agreement between nations without interference or confrontation from either side, resulting in securing accurate information with no loss of aircraft or life. The President, skeptical of the acceptance of the proposal by the Soviets, said, "I'll give it one shot, if they don't accept it then we will fly the plane." Lt. Col. Richard Sully Leghorn, a USAF reconnaissance pilot, worked as a consultant to President Eisenhower's Assistant for Disarmament Affairs during 1955-56, and was instrumental in formulating the "Open Skies" proposal.

The French and British expressed interest in the policy, but as expected, the Soviets rejected any plan that would subject them to surveillance by a Western power. As a result of the Soviets rejection, a new reconnaissance plane strategy had to become a reality. Considering the many strategic military and political problems which could be associated with the project, the research team known as "the Land Panel" made a recommendation to President Eisenhower to put a civilian agency rather than the military to head the project. Its reasoning was that, if a civilian plane was downed in Soviet territory, it could mean the difference of being construed as spying, and not an act of war. As the Supreme Allied Commander during WWII, President Eisenhower understood the need to maintain vigilance over potential adversaries and avoid any perception of starting a war, and agreed the CIA should have the supervision and coordination authority. Consequently, Richard M. Bissell of the CIA, an MIT PhD., was given the responsibility for one of the most ambitious and secret programs in the CIA, project Aquatone. Kelly Johnson and his Lockheed Skunk Works team designed, developed, and constructed the first CL-282. Kelly was a man of his word. In July 1955 he delivered the first plane, under budget, in just nine months. Initially, the decision to develop and use the CL-282 was not unanimous. It is said that General Curtis LeMay, Commander of the Strategic Air Command (SAC) walked out of a CL-282 presentation, saying he was not interested in a plane without wheels or guns.

The aircraft needed an official name. If the plane was not to be a military plane, that eliminated the ability to use military terminology to designate the plane, and not wanting to associate the plane with its objective of spying, the decision was made to simply refer to it as a "utility" plane. Utility was non-descript identifier and could easily be passed off as a weather observation plane if necessary. Since designations U-1 and U-3 were already in use, U-2 seemed to be the logical choice. So, the CL-282 became the U-2 and was referred to as such from that point on. The U-2 became affectionately known as the "Dragon Lady." The name "Dragon" was the unclassified name used by the SAC in the formation of the first squadron to fly the U-2. Others say it was because at that time the U-2 was considered the most difficult plane to fly. Take off, in-flight maneuvering and landing was enough to make a pilot foul-tempered, but once airborne, just flying the plane was a pleasure. Thus, the saying among U-2 pilots was that, "You must fight the dragon before you could dance with the lady." Pilot Captain Francis Gary Powers states in his book *Operation Overflight, A Memoir of the U-2 Incident*; "It was not an easy plane to fly, but it was not dangerous." Greg Nelson, a Lockheed Martin U-2 Senior Test Pilot put it this way, "It's a survival contest between you and the jet, and you don't want the jet to win." In a phone interview with Retired USAF Major Greg Kimbrough, a U-2 pilot 2000 through 2009 during Operation Enduring Freedom, he said that even though the updated U-2 plane has a larger frame, a more efficient engine, and a computerized instrument panel, it remains a fragile, difficult-to-fly dragon in a dangerous environment, but fun.

9

THE REYNOLDS WRAP® PLANE

The U-2 was a unique aircraft design incorporating the profile of a traditional glider, with long seventy plus foot tapered wings which gave it added lift and additional fuel storage. These long wings also gave it the ability to glide extended distances, should the need arise. An article published on the Interesting Engineering website relates a story that during one test flight over the state of Tennessee, a U-2 suffered an un-recoverable engine flame-out. The pilot was able to glide and reach Kirtland Air Force base in Albuquerque, New Mexico some 1200 miles away. These long wings compared to its overall fifty-foot length made it look somewhat gangly, but they provided the capacity to hold 1,350 gallons of fuel, enough to cover some 4,000 to 5,000 nautical miles. Today, the wingspan of the U-2 is 103 feet with a total wing area of 1,000 square feet. By comparison, at thirty-two feet in length, the wing area of an F-16 Fighting Falcon is only 300 square feet. In his book *Secret Empire*, author Phillip Taubman states that USAF pilot Martin Knutson, who was one of the first pilots selected for the U-2 program, had formed a mental picture of a sleek, futuristic, supersonic designed plane. However, when he got his first look at the oddly shaped plane he said, "I don't want anything to do with this damn thing." Knutson said he changed his attitude after he flew the plane. "I found out it was no kid's toy. It was going to take a lot of skill to handle this machine" he said.

Kelly Johnson's specifications called for the use of light weight material such as aluminum whenever possible. Every pound in weight would effectively reduce the altitude by one foot, and because it was designed to operate at 70,000 feet, every pound saved was significant. At an empty weight of some 13,000 pounds, it was one third the weight of a normal plane. Because of its missions, Lockheed built the U-2 to meet Kelly Johnson's specifications, not military aircraft specifications or handling qualities, although it would be flown by military pilots.

The Kelly team jokingly referred to the plane as being made of Reynolds Wrap®, and that was not far from being true. To make the aircraft light, its aluminum skin was only 0.02 inches thick making it very fragile requiring careful handling on the ground. One pilot made the observation that if you picked up the end of a wing tip, it would bend. The plane required even more careful handling in the air. If the U-2 was flown too slow it could stall, and if it was flown too fast, the wings could literally tear off. Adding one more complication to the equation, speed too slow at one altitude was too fast at another altitude. Its shorter tapered body and an extended wing span made the U-2 difficult to maneuver and slow to turn, creating vulnerability to anti-aircraft missiles. The plane, powered by a single Pratt & Whitney J57-P-13 non-after burning turbojet engine, was meant to overcome these weaknesses through its ability to operate at flight levels above 70,000 feet, and a speed close to Mach 1 (the speed of sound, or "Mach," is 769.7 mph.). Sustained flight at this altitude and speed was unimaginable during this time. These U-2 pilots were literary flying into unknown territory.

A motion picture titled *Toward the Unknown* premiered in 1956 starring William Holden, Lloyd Nolan, and Virginia Leith, and the screen debut of James Garner. The movie plot was about the experimental Bell X-1's record of flying into unknown space faster than the speed of sound. That movie title was representative of the environment in which these U-2 pilots were operating, so it seemed appropriate to adopt "Toward the Unknown" as a squadron motto. The phrase accurately described the program and the squadron team members overwhelmingly approved it. The motto was developed into a flight suit sleeve patch, which is still worn by U-2 personnel today.

The Lockheed aeronautical engineers believed an aircraft flying Mach 1 at 70,000 feet would be beyond the reach of the Soviet's radar tracking and Surface-to-Air Missiles (SAM), and the MiG-19, the Soviet's best interceptor fighter, which could just reach 45,000 feet. Not so. Unlike the United States, the Soviet Union had improved its radar technology after WWII, and could track aircraft flying above 65,000 feet. Adding to their missile arsenal, the Soviets developed a specialized type SAM referred to as a SA-2 Guideline, specifically designed to bring down high-flying aircraft.

Unfortunately, for greater reconnaissance effectiveness, planes like the U-2 flew a straight-line flight plan making them a more predictable target. Detection on radar was inevitable in most cases, even at these high altitudes. When the Soviet early radar warning system detected an incoming object, the SAM sites begin sweeping the sky. Once a location was confirmed and the aircraft determined to be a threat, the site fired a SAM, usually with precision accuracy. Despite its accuracy and speed, SAC information indicated that because of its 60,000-foot ceiling, even the SA-2 missile could not reach the U-2 flying at its 70,000 plus feet working flight level.

10

THE U-2 NEW REQUIREMENTS

In addition to all the problems and red tape in getting the U-2 project approved, a new set of problems emerged in the development and production of the aircraft. Because of the uniqueness of the CL-282-U-2 missions, relying on normal aircraft design and functionality was of little value. This was an aircraft which would fly higher and faster than any plane in existence at that time, and would subject the plane and its pilot to extremes never encountered before. Therefore, many changes were required and creativity was the challenge for the Lockheed team. Volumes could be written about these new requirements, but here are a few of the most significant requirements Kelly's Lockheed Skunk Works® team faced in the development of the CL-282-U-2.

A NEW ENGINE

Kelley's original design for the CL-282 was to be powered by the General Electric J73 engine, the type used in the USAF F-86 H Saber jet. With a thrust of 9,000 lbf (pounds of force), a J73 engine powered an F-86H to a world's speed record of 649.302 mph in 1954. However, with the need to deliver speeds close to Mach 1 on a sustained basis, the Air Force had concerns about the future performance of the General Electric engine. An agreement was reached, and the final approval of the joint USAF-CIA project came with the provision that the engine be changed to the more reliable Pratt and Whitney J57 engine. The J57, produced from 1951 to 1965, was a twin-spool, sixteen-stage axial flow turbojet engine developed in the early 1950s, and the first American jet engine to produce more than 10,000 lbs. thrust. This successful high-performance engine was also used in the F-100 Super Sabre, Convair F-102 Delta Dart, Republic F-105 prototype, and an experimental Boeing B-47B. The JP-57 consistently delivered the speed and reliability needed for the U-2.

New Type Fuel

In addition to the new engine and the altitude at which it would function, the JP-8 fuel normally used in jet aircraft would not perform at the U-2's sustained high altitudes, so a new fuel was needed. The Shell Oil® company developed a Jet Propellant Thermally Stable (JPTS) JP-7 fuel, which had a lower freeze point, higher viscosity, and higher thermal stability than standard Air Force jet fuels. The JP-7 fuel had limited availability and the cost was over three times the per-gallon price of the Air Force's primary jet fuel. The JP7 fuel was needed, so the cost of the fuel was no obstacle.

New Flight Instruments

Instrument recalibration was another problem. Because aircrafts in use at that time had a much lower ceiling of some 45,000 feet, a new altimeter was necessary for the U-2. To ensure the project continued in its top-secret project status, the CIA devised a cover story involving the development of an experimental rocket aircraft when Kelly Johnson ordered altimeters calibrated to 80,000 feet.

New Pilot Selection Process

Because the U-2 was a new plane with new capabilities and new objectives, the CIA realized the need for a new pilot selection process. This was a top-secret program and mistakes could jeopardize our national security. Therefore, it was necessary that the pilots selected meet the highest standards physically, mentally and emotionally. The USAF agreed to shoulder the responsibility for pilots and went to great lengths in selecting, testing and training these pilots. Each candidate was subjected to an interview process to evaluate his self-confidence, professionalism and airmanship on the ground and in the air. If they passed the interview process, they continued with medical tests which have been described as exhaustive and often painful, and then on to the mental testing which was very intense. If they made it through all this testing, they were considered worthy for flight training.

The flight suit normally worn by pilots was insufficient for the U-2 pilot. Because the U-2 was to operate at 65,000 to 70,000 feet, and the cockpit was to be pressurized only to an altitude equivalency of 28,000 to 30,000 feet, a pressurized suit was necessary. James Paget Henry, an Assistant Professor of aviation medicine at the University of Southern California, developed the prototype partial pressure suit using a separate oxygen mask to provide pressurized oxygen. To counter balance the opposing pressure on the breathing pressure necessary to prevent hypoxia at high altitudes, Henry included a series of small rubber tubes, called capstans, within the pressure suit and inflated them. The pressurized suit and mask provided the pilot's oxygen supply and a margin of safety in the event cabin pressure was lost. Henry's pressure suit design worked and was subsequently perfected by the David Clark Company into the S-1 flight suit which continued to be worn by U-2 and SR-71A pilots.

A support team, the Physiological Support Division (PSD), was formed to maintain the new pressure suit and equipment, and assist pilots. The first PSD was established by the Air Force 11 June 1957 at Laughlin AFB, Texas to service the U-2 program. The PSD Technicians were assigned the responsibility for the flight crew member's safety before, during and after a mission as it related to the pressure suit and life support systems. They assisted the pilot in getting into this bulky pressure suit and connecting it to the U-2's life support systems before the flight. The process was reversed after the mission was completed and the aircraft was safely back at the base. A more comprehensive discussion of the PSD process is included in Chapter 26, Getting Suited-Up.

The importance of maintaining the pressure suit in excellent condition, and ensuring good life support system connections cannot be over emphasized. The goal of the PSD Technicians was a no-fail, zero-defect mission. Retired USAF Major Greg Kimbrough, a U-2 pilot 2000 through 2009 related his story of returning home after flying a long-duration reconnaissance sortie over Iraq during Enduring Freedom in late 2002. At 60,000-70,000 feet a faulty seal on his face mask caused him to begin a decompression process. High altitude decompression sickness is caused by the formation of nitrogen gas bubbles in the blood, known to deep-sea divers as the bends. The condition can be very painful and can trigger neurological effects because the bubbles lodge in the body anywhere from joints and lungs to the spinal cord and brain. Experiencing severe headaches, nausea, stiffing joints and some frostbite due to the loss of pressure, Major Kimbrough said he completed the sortie and returned to base although unable to read the small print on the instruments, numbers, or even recognize his landing field. With the assistance of ground-controlled approach radar assistance, Major Kimbrough safely landed his plane. "I'm not sure just how I did that, but I did," he said.

New Pilot In-Flight Dining and Drinking Process

A normal mission could last up to nine hours, and the loss of fluid in the body during an extended flight was something new to be addressed. Indications are, even with food and drink available, a pilot could lose up to six pounds in an eight-hour flight. The nourishment issue was solved by developing food and liquid in tube form. The pilot's helmet contained a small self-sealing port through which a long feeding tube could be inserted and with a few squeezes, refreshing food or drink could be consumed. The periodic hydration during the flight was needed, but it created additional fluid. The fluid excretion problem was originally solved by using a catheter, but that became uncomfortable as the pilot moved around on a long flight, so an external bladder was added permitting the ability to urinate while sitting. A more detailed discussion about how this process worked is included in Chapter 26, Getting Suited Up.

New Pre-Flight Plane Procedures

The pre-flight procedures for the U-2 are a bit different from those of any other plane. The readiness of the U-2 aircraft and the safety of the pilot are the responsibility of the Crew Chief. There are two crew chiefs for each flight working in two groups: the preparation and launch group, and recovery and inspection group.

Pre-flight preparation begins some five hours before the scheduled takeoff. The Preparation and Launch group start the process by removing all of the protective covers placed on the aircraft while it is parked. The plane power is turned on to ensure the lights, gauges and oxygen system are functioning properly. Fuel tanks are checked for the correct quantity of fuel, and the wing balance is verified for flight. The check is completed by ensuring there are no foreign objects or debris in the engine intakes. Once completed, the crew chiefs certify the aircraft ready to fly.

For other aircraft, the pilot and the co-pilot conduct a series of walk-around inspections and external systems check before takeoff. This customary preflight process would no longer work for the U-2 pilot because the pressurized flight suit is bulky, limits mobility, reduces dexterity, and causes rapid heat buildup with physical activity. Once the pilot arrives at the aircraft, he immediately settles into the cockpit and is attached to the oxygen and air-cooling systems. The Crew Chief then begins the final launch procedures.

About one hour before launch the launch group does a foreign object debris (FOD) walk on the entire ramp to ensure it is safe for the aircraft to take off. After the final inspection procedures are completed and the plane has been cleared to fly, the plane is pushed out of the hangar and released for the six-to ten-hour mission.

New Pre-Flight Pilot Procedure

The pre-flight procedure for other pilots involves dressing into their flight suit and attending a flight briefing. However, because of the nature of their flight, the pilots of the U-2 were subjected to a more rigorous process. This process began twenty-four hours prior to a flight by restricting their diet to high protein, low residue meals which can be almost completely absorbed through the gastrointestinal tract. The CIA produced a manual to instruct pilots on the preferred diet for "physical maintenance control," including the pre-flight diet and regimen. Thanks to the Task & Purpose website and the Freedom of Information Act, we have the dietary information from the CIA manual.

The 1962 CIA manual for "physical maintenance control" outlined the following from the pre-flight diet and regimen of pilots:

> The basis for such a diet is meat, rice, eggs, sugar, small amounts of fruit juices, tea, and coffee. Foods allowed are as follows:
>
> a. Beverages: carbonated, coffee, tea.
> b. Cereals and cereal products: rice, cream of wheat, noodles, macaroni.

c. Cheese: cottage.

d. Desserts: gelatin, sherbet, angel food cake, sponge cake, sugar cookies.

e. Eggs: soft or hard cooked, scrambled, poached.

f. Fat: butter or margarine, not in excess of three tablespoons per day.

g. Fruit: strained juice, canned, peeled fruit such as peaches or pears, limited amounts.

h. Meat: fowl, fish, beef, veal, liver, chicken, fish (baked or broiled).

i. Soups: clear broth with rice or noodles.

j. Sweets: sugar, jelly, hard candies (in limited amounts).

k. Vegetables: strained, such as tomatoes, peas, carrots, potatoes (baked or boiled); not over one serving per day.

Foods to avoid entirely during the twenty-four-hour pre-flight period of feeding of the low residue diet are these:

a. Beverages: milk and milk drinks.

b. Breads: coarse or whole grain.

c. Cereals and cereal products: whole grain, popcorn.

d. Cheese: all cheeses, except cottage.

e. Crackers: whole grain

f. Desserts: all rich desserts, such as pies and pastries.

g. Fats: in excess of three tablespoons per day.

h. Fried foods: all.

i. Fruits: all, except strained fruit juice and canned, peeled fruit, such as peaches or pears.

j. Meat: fowl, fish, if fatty (such as goose or mackerel), fat pork, any tough cuts of meat, lamb and mutton.

k. Nuts

l. Pickles

m. Soups: creamy or spicy.

n. Spices, condiments and highly seasoned foods.

o. Sweets: jams and marmalades; avoid all sugar and sweets in excess.

p. Vegetables: all except strained vegetables such as tomatoes, peas, carrots, and baked or boiled potatoes.

Between-meal snacks or drinks other than carbonated beverages, coffee, tea, or clear soups, should be avoided.

To prepare for a nine-hour mission at an environment similar to that at 30,000 feet, the pilot dressed in the pressure suit and spent an hour before the flight breathing 100% oxygen in a special chamber. When this was completed, the pilot was shuttled to the aircraft. The PSD Technicians assisted the pilot getting into the aircraft and hooked up all his life support and communication systems.

The U-2 Operating Locations usually prohibited a pilot from flying for 48 hours after a flight to allow time for his body to recuperate from the physically demanding mission.

New Takeoff and Landing Methodology

Takeoff and landing of the U-2 were another two challenging problems. To reduce weight and drag, the decision was made to eliminate the standard takeoff and landing equipment. The original design called for the plane to take off from a special cart and land on its belly, but realizing the potential for plane damage, a revision was necessary. Instead of the standard three landing wheels, one under each wing and a third at the rear fuselage, the U-2 had a bicycle configuration. A forward set of wheels located just behind the cockpit, and a rear set of wheels located behind the engine which were coupled to the rudder providing the ability to steer during taxiing. To stabilize the plane while taxiing and take-off, two auxiliary wheels called "pogos" were used. A pogo wheel fit into a socket located under each wing at about mid-span, and would separate and drop out as the plane lifted into the air.

The Recovery and Inspection group begin the preparation for recovering the aircraft about thirty minutes prior to landing. As the U-2 lands, it is followed by a chase car assisting the pilot with information and instructions as the aircraft descends. As with the takeoff, the plane cannot maintain balance on its two wheels while landing, so each wingtip had a titanium skid attached to it. As the plane slowed, one wing would drag on the runway surface until the plane came to a stop, then the ground crew re-attached the pogo wheels to the wings providing the ability for the aircraft to taxi. This was a somewhat unorthodox landing process, but it accomplishes all the needs.

Once the aircraft has been towed into the hangar, the pilot provides information on any issue encountered during the flight, and the Recovery and Inspection group conducts a post-flight inspection of the aircraft for its next flight. After the inspection is complete and the necessary maintenance has been performed, the aircraft is refueled, parked and covered, ready for its next mission.

New Cameras

The cameras used for aerial photography prior to the U-2 produced photos without a significant amount of close-up detail. The Trimetrogon K-17 system was the most used and consisted of three cameras for three different angle shots. The K-17 cameras produced a resolution of twenty to twenty-five feet at 33,000 feet, and while that was acceptable, it was not capable of clear photography at higher altitudes. The goal of the U-2 was to produce photos with a resolution of ten feet which meant new cameras. The Air Force used a K-18 camera and had other cameras with longer focal lengths, but they were too large and heavy to use in the U-2.

After consideration the decision was made to use a modified version of the K-38, a twenty-four-inch system produced by the Hycon Manufacturing Company, and renamed the A-1 camera by the CIA. The A-1 was eventually replaced by the B-1, a thirty-six-inch medium wide lens which produced high-definition photographs. The film was fed into the cameras using spools and each spool contained some 6,500 feet of film, or over a mile of film. Photographs taken at 60,000 feet yielded detail of objects as small as 2.5 feet. Although the cameras continued to be perfected over time, the B-1 was a good start.

To demonstrate the ability and effectiveness of the new plane and camera, CIA Agency Chief Richard Bissell instructed a U-2 to fly over President Eisenhower's farm in Pennsylvania and photograph it at 60,000 feet. Viewing the photos, the President was astonished that not only could he see his cattle, but also their feeding troughs. "This is close to incredible," he stated. The photos taken by a U-2 during the Cuban missile crisis in 1962, and shown to President Kennedy reflects the resolution detail of the camera. One of these photos is included on page 105.

The U-2 was the prototype for high-altitude reconnaissance and several of the equipment processes and procedures established for the U-2 plane and its pilot remain in use today. The U-2 was replaced by the SR-

71A Blackbird, which became the premier reconnaissance plane during the Cold War. A significant amount detail relating to the processes and details are included in the SR-71A Blackbird section.

11

AREA 51,
EXPERIMENTAL AIRCRAFT TESTING

WARNING
TOP SECRET RESEARCH FACILITY
USE OF DEADLY FORCE AUTHORIZED

AREA 51

Restricted Area
It is unlawful to enter this area without permission of the installation commander.
Sec. 21, Internal Security Act of 1950; 50 U.S.C. 797

While on this installation all personnel and the property under their control are subject to search and seizure.

Photography Prohibited
It is unlawful to make any photograph, film, map, sketch, picture, drawing, graphic representation of this area or equipment at or flying over this installation.
Sec. 21, Internal Security Act of 1950; 18 U.S.C. 795

Use of deadly force authorized.

(Courtesy CIA)

Before the CL-282 project began, Kelly Johnson knew the Lockheed build site in Palmdale, California was not suitable for adequately testing the plane. He had to find a remote location and meet several CIA non-negotiable requirements. It must have a useable airstrip sufficient to accommodate the plane, be completely away from the public and capable of being fully secured with limited access from air or land traffic, but within reasonable commuting distance from the Lockheed plant. After considering several options, the abandoned site just north of Las Vegas was chosen. It would take a lot of work and money to make it operational, but this site, named Area 51, met all the requirements.

Area 51 in Nevada is well known today because of the many UFO sighting stories and alien conspiracy theories published over the years, but in 1955 very little was known about it. In fact, its official existence was not acknowledged until 2013. Area 51 was classified as a remote detachment of Edwards Air Force Base, California with a specific purpose of developing weapon systems and testing experimental aircraft such as the U-2. My research indicated that in addition to the U-2, A-12 and SR-71A, several stealth aircraft including the F-22 Raptor, B-2 and the F-117 Night Hawk have been developed and tested in the airspace of the Nevada desert. Declassified CIA documents also reveal Area 51's role in a project named "Have Doughnut," which was a study of a covertly obtained Soviet MiG-21 Fishbed-E. The US acquired the MiG in 1967 from Israel after an Iraqi Air Force pilot flew it into Israel in a pre-arranged defection.

As it was in 1955, Area 51 has remained a highly secured area displaying signs around the perimeter which advise that unauthorized access is strictly prohibited, with deadly force authorized against trespassers. Additionally, the twenty-three by twenty-five miles airspace above it is also restricted airspace. Area 51 continues to be in the forefront of military technology development.

Area 51 was developed by the CIA in April 1955 as Project Aquatone, to test the Lockheed U-2. Located in a salt flat called Groom Lake, Area 51 was also used as an aerial gunnery range for World War II Army pilots. With its remote location and usable airstrip, the site was perfect for U-2 testing and pilot training. However, the first challenge was how to get the U-2 from the California developmental plant to the Nevada facility. The decision was made to transport the U-2 in pieces to Area 51 via a C-124 Globemaster, the primary heavy-lift transport for the USAF Military Air Transportation Service (MATS). The U-2 was disassembled at the Lockheed plant in California, flown to Area 51, and re-constructed.

When the A-12 Oxcart was under development in 1960 to replace the U-2, Area 51 was again used for testing and pilot training. Many of the UFO stories we have read about were in all reality, the testing of the U-2 and the A-12. Because of project secrecy, the CIA and USAF could not reveal the details of this testing to the public. So, "natural phenomena" or "high-altitude weather research" became the standard explanation for a reported UFO sighting.

Although the A-12 was designed, fabricated, and assembled at plant number 42 in Palmdale, California, engineers knew from the beginning that flight testing, final development, and pilot training would require another location. Because the A-12 Oxcart was a CIA project, they determined Area 51's remote and classified location along with its restricted air space, provided the secrecy required for the Oxcart project.

As with the U-2, this location change necessitated transporting the A-12 from Palmdale to Area 51. The decision was made to transport the plane overland. First, the highway route was determined, surveyed and cleared of any obstacles including: narrow passageways, road signs, trees and large rocks. This clearing work began in 1959 and the travel route was ready for the first trip in February 1962.

Next, two shipping type steel frame boxes were built to transport the plane. The largest box was 105 feet long and 35 feet wide and carried the central part of the plane. The remaining pieces were carried in the smaller box. These container boxes, which far exceeded the California and Nevada highway transportation standards at that time, were hoisted onto special Lockheed tractor trailer flatbed trucks. Because of the extended length of the larger box, the trailer was equipped with remote independent rear wheel steering similar to the steering on a large hook and ladder fire truck. The first trip started on 26 February 1962 and took three days to complete. Three additional trips were made in 1962 and by 1964, the remaining A-12s arrived at Area 51.

Anticipating the increased air activity in the area would generate concern and potential problems, in January 1962 the Federal Aviation Agency (FAA) approved an expansion in the restricted air space above Area 51, and specific FAA air traffic controllers were assigned to the project. To further ensure secrecy, the North American Air Defense Command implemented new procedures, which prevented their radar station from reporting the detection of this high-altitude plane.

The testing went well until CIA personnel discovered that Soviet spy satellites were making regular reconnaissance passes over Nevada. Something was up and the Soviets wanted to know what. The CIA ascertained the satellite's pass-over schedule and provided the information to Area 51 personnel. Based on the schedule, any outside testing was interrupted and the A-12 was moved into a nearby building. After the satellite passed, the plane was pulled from the building and testing resumed. This process, although necessary, was labor intensive and quite annoying.

If that was not a sufficient problem, electronic counter measure specialists determined that the shape of the A-12 could be revealed through its shadow. When a plane was in the hot desert sun for any length of time, its shadow created a cooler temperature than the space on which the plane was parked. Therefore, the Soviet satellite cameras could produce an infrared shape of the plane based on the temperature difference. Because the temperature could not be controlled, area testing crews constructed fake plane shapes out of cardboard to cast misleading shadows in an attempt to fool the infrared satellites. The Soviets, despite all their efforts, never solved the secrets of A-12 Oxcart before the program became public in the mid-1960s, and notwithstanding all the CIA's work, the A-12 was never involved in spy work over the Soviet Union. Just as the A-12 was declared reconnaissance mission ready, its successor, the US Air Force's famed SR-71A Blackbird was already being designed.

The CIA knew all too well it would be impossible to keep the U-2 a secret forever. Given a sufficient number of flights, the possibility of leaked information, a crash, or problem during flight was inevitable. To avoid unnecessary publicity or speculation, the U-2 was introduced in April 1956 as a plane developed jointly by Lockheed and the USAF Air Weather Service specifically for the purpose of studying weather related flying issues, and in fact, it did some of this type work. The program including the pilots would be under the oversight of not the military, but the National Advisory Committee on Aeronautics (NACA) which later became the National Aeronautics and Space Administration (NASA). This introduction as a weather service plane seemed to satisfy any curiosity and the U-2 continued its reconnaissance missions for the next four years without public concern. However, on 1 May 1960, that all changed when the Soviets shot down Gary Power's U-2 over Sverdlovsk, Russia.

State Map Identifying Location of Area 51.

Area 51.
(Courtesy Google Earth)

12

THE U-2 INCIDENT
OVER SVERDLOVSK, RUSSIA

From its introduction in 1956 until the Powers flight in 1960, the U-2 had flown twenty-four reconnaissance missions into Soviet air space, many of these under the CIA's "we must know" approach, but President Eisenhower had given his approval reluctantly. In the spring of 1956, the Office of Scientific Intelligence issued a study indicating Soviet detection was probable, contradicting the CIA's assurance to the president. Knowing the Soviets were aware of the U-2 flights and could track them on radar, the president was very concerned that eventually a plane would be shot down. However, the results of these missions proved to be worth the risk. The photos showed new Soviet missile launch sites under development and deployment, demonstrating to many people the necessity to continue flights. As 1959 rolled around, Kelly Johnson had started modifying the U-2 by using a more powerful engine, the Pratt and Whitney J75-P13 anticipating it would provide a greater measure of safety for the missions. The president was torn between dealing with the intense criticism over the perception that the US had fallen behind the Soviets in the development of missiles, the need for the U-2 program to remain active but highly secret and covert, and the increasing chance that a Soviet missile would shoot down a plane. Realizing that the odds were stacking up against continuing successful U-2 flights, one more mission was authorized. This would be a mission involving more aggressive flying into Soviet airspace than any previous flight.

In April 1960, the first reconnaissance mission, Sortie Number 4154, to fly completely across the Soviet Union, some 2900 miles, was approved by the president and scheduled. Some people speculate that the president gave his approval without being fully aware of the increased Soviet threat, and anticipated neither plane nor the pilot would survive if the plane was shot down. In my phone conversation with Gary Powers Jr, he stated that with twenty-seven sorties over the Soviet Union, the most hours and experience of any U-2 pilot, his dad, Captain Francis Gary Powers, was selected to fly this mission. The U-2 planes were flown on a rotation basis and the plane Captain Powers expected to fly had reached its maximum allowable flying hours and was grounded for a maintenance check. The substitute U-2, Article 360, 56–6693, was flown in on Saturday before his scheduled Sunday mission. Knowing the history of U-2 360, Captain Powers was somewhat dismayed describing it as "A dog, never having flown exactly right. Something was always going wrong, including a fuel tank problem, and occasionally an autopilot malfunction." Nevertheless, it was the plane selected for Sortie Number 4154 on 1 May 1960.

The flight plan called for a 0600 take-off from Peshawar, Pakistan, overfly Afghanistan and the Hindu Kush mountain range, cross the Soviet Union, to the Barents Sea, and along the northern coast of Norway. Factoring in the time changes, the plane should land in Bodo, Norway about nightfall. Interestingly, Bodo was not only the landing destination for this U-2 flight, it later served as an emergency recovery base for all European SR-71A flights, and five Blackbirds landed there from 1981 to 1985. Sortie Number 4154 was to cover a total of some 3,800 miles and last nine hours. Unfortunately, one weakness of the U-2 was that it was impossible to make the exhaust ducts stealthy and about four hours into the flight the U-2, cruising between 65,000 and 70,000 feet, was detected on Russian radar and forced downed by a near miss SA-2 Guideline missile near Sverdlovsk, present-day Yekaterinburg, Russia.

Although there are conflicting stories concerning how the U-2 was impacted by the missile, the official SAC story indicates that after radar detection, the Soviets sent up a plane, probably a MiG-19, to fire a missile at the U-2, while simultaneously continuing to fire SA-2 Guideline SAMs. One of the eight ground-to-air missiles fired at the U-2 hit the Soviet MiG and the explosion shock waves were so severe, the U-2's fragile wings fractured and broke off. Another account of the incident says the U-2 received a direct hit from a second missile, while beginning to plummet downward. Several months after being shot down, the Soviets permitted Captain Powers to view the plane wreckage and he stated, "Everything I saw confirmed my belief that the aircraft had not been hit, but disabled by a near-miss." In his book, *Operation Overflight*, Captain Powers states, "I heard a dull thump and a tremendous orange flash lit the cockpit and sky." Having no control of the aircraft, he assumed it was because of a broken control cable, or the tail section was completely gone. Regardless of the specific undetermined problem, the U-2 began falling and spinning with the nose pointing up. Unable to engage the ejection seat for fear of severing his legs on the canopy rails, Captain Powers unlocked and released the canopy, climbed out of the plane and parachuted to the ground. Although he retained the US silver dollar poison pin, he opted not to use it hoping somehow his chances to escape was a better alternative than suicide. Unlike Captain Powers, U-2 pilots today no longer carry the cyanide capsule or the US silver dollar, containing a curare covered poison pin to use in case of capture.

On the ground, he was apprehended and transported to the city of Sverdlovsk and turned over to the Russian police, most likely the KGB. Because Captain Powers had been unable to reach the destruct switches as he exited the aircraft, the Soviets were now in possession of the U-2 wreckage, In August 1960, Captain Powers was convicted of espionage in a for-show public trial and served almost two years in the Vladimir Russian prison before being exchanged for the KGB spy Rudolf Abel in 1962. This exchange was the inspiration for the 2015 Steven Spielberg movie *Bridge of Spies* starring Tom Hanks and Mark Rylance, which dramatized the negotiations for the exchange of Powers for Abel. In a presentation to the American Legion Post 31, Tuscumbia, Alabama, Gary Powers Jr. stated that he served as a technical consultant on the movie to help ensure the accuracy of the event. The Powers U-2 incident would become a major diplomatic crisis for the US and a notable setback for the US reconnaissance program. President Dwight Eisenhower eventually admitted, "Almost from the very beginning, we learned that the Soviets knew about the [U-2] flights...." With the Soviets aware of the U-2 overflights, and the ability to track it on radar, it was just matter of time before they would solve their SAM missile-guidance problem, creating extreme vulnerability for the U-2.

The explanation for how the plane was shot down was questioned by many concerned citizens, and for several years there was substantial conjecture and several conspiracy theories. These theories involved everything from CIA intervention, to an NSA cryptologist defection, to the involvement of double agents. However, the theory I found most interesting implicates a person very familiar to most people, Lee Harvey

Oswald, the accused assassin of President John F. Kennedy in 1963.

Oswald, a former US Marine Corp. radar technician and an avowed Marxist, renounced his US citizenship in October 1959 and proposed to Soviet officials that if he were granted Soviet citizenship, he would provide them information concerning the Marine Corps. The knowledge he acquired from his duty assignments was fairly extensive, including operational details about several military bases. He also intimated to the Soviets that he might know something of "special interest" he could share with them. That special interest information was speculated to be about the U-2.

The Naval Air Facility Atsugi, in Tokyo, Japan, was home to several type planes including the U-2. Oswald was stationed at Atsugi from September 1957 to November 1958, and through his security clearance, he would have probably tracked the U-2 on radar. Whether or not Oswald had sufficient information which would help the Soviets shoot down a U-2 remains debatable, and based on his job responsibilities, there was only a slight possibility he possessed this type information. Other people however, doubt that statement. Six months after Oswald renounced his citizenship and made his offer to the Soviets, Captain Powers' U-2 was shot down. For some theorists, that was more than just a coincidence. Among the many documents produced by the Warren Commission investigating President Kennedy's Assignation was No. 931 titled, "Oswald's Access to Information About the U-2."

13

AN EPIC ENDING
FROM A NEW BEGINNING

A total of 104 U-2 planes were produced and operated by either the CIA or the USAF, depending on mission parameters. Each plane was custom built and unique. The U-2 was designed as a land-based plane; that is, it took off on land; flew its mission and returned to land, and was not designed for air-to-air refueling. In May 1961 Lockheed was requested to modify some CIA and USAF U-2s to provide air refueling capability using a KC-97 or KC-135-Stratotanker. This successful air-to-air refueling modification extended the flying range from 4,000 miles to 8,000 miles and flying time to more than 14 hours.

Always looking for ways to increase its range and flexibility, in 1963 the Office of Special Activities initiated Project Whale Tale to determine whether or not the U-2 could operate from a carrier. Unfortunately, the procedure was fraught with logistical problems unique to the U-2. First, the pogo wheels used to balance the plane would not work on the carrier. Flight line personnel had to hold up each wing tip as the pilot powered up, and let go when the aircraft catapult started to accelerate the aircraft plane to launch speed. Second, the long wings made it difficult to maneuver and store the plane and third, because the plane was designed as a glider, it did not want to stop on the deck runway. On the first test landing, when the tail hook caught the wire, the aircraft pitched nose-down, resulting in damage to the nose. Unable to overcome these obstacles, Project Whale Tail was scuttled. The U-2 performed only one operational mission from the carrier USS *Ranger* in May 1964, and became only a footnote in the Cold War history books

As a side project, the CIA and the USAF continued to work on the reconnaissance satellite Corona Project with little success. The Project was beset with numerous operational, navigation and camera problems, and doubtful to ever become a reality. Even when the satellite worked properly the photos produced were without sufficient clarity and detail needed for a good assessment. Although the risk of being detected was great, the CIA had no choice but to rely on the U-2 as the primary spy plane. During the Cuba crisis, satellite photos were determined to be of little use because of the lack of detail and the time necessary to develop and produce the film. Bud Wheelon, head of the CIA Office of Scientific Intelligence complained they needed the data back that day not a month from now, and the U-2 was capable of delivering detailed photos quickly.

Colonel Oleg Penkovsky, a top-ranking officer in the Soviet Intelligence Services was a double agent who also spied for the US and Britain. The primary reason Colonel Penkovsky spied for the United States and Britain was in retaliation for being defamed and slandered by other Soviet officers because of his father's political stand during the Russian Civil War. After informing the United States about the presence of Soviet nuclear missiles in Cuba, U-2s were dispatched to survey the threat and provide data in a short time frame. Until then, the US had little reason to conduct regular surveillance flights over Cuba, and if the Soviet Union's plan to quickly get the missiles in place and activated had worked, it would have been too late for the US to do anything, even if they were detected.

Through photographs taken by a U-2 in October 1962, the CIA's National Photographic Interpretation Center (NPIC) confirmed that medium range Soviet ballistic missiles were being placed in Cuba. One of the early photographs taken during U-2 reconnaissance flights over Cuba and presented to President Kennedy is on page 99.

Working with the CIA and MI6, Colonel Penkovsky helped the NPIC analyst to correctly identify the type of missiles on the U-2 imagery as Russian missiles. He provided detailed information about the launch sites confirming that US missile systems were far more advanced than the Soviet Union's. Colonel Penkovsky's information came only three days before the missiles became fully functional, thereby giving President Kennedy limited time to respond. The subsequent action of President Kennedy resulted in a naval blockade of Cuba and the removal of all Soviet missiles. In retrospect, this incident was one which brought the world closer that it had ever been to a nuclear war. In the opinion of many historians, the direction of the

Cold War changed dramatically because of Colonel Penkovsky's action relating to Cuba. He was arrested by the Soviet KGB on 22 October 1962 and sentenced to death after a highly publicized trial. He was executed in May 1963.

On 27 October 1962, another U-2, flown by SAC pilot Major Rudolf Anderson Jr., was shot down over Cuba by a Soviet SA-2 missile killing him and destroying the plane. With the loss of two U-2 planes, it became evident that a new spy plane was necessary. Surprised by no one, the design for a new plane came from none other than Kelly Johnson. Although the concept was difficult to comprehend by politicians, and most military personnel, Kelly was proposing a plane which could cruse at more than three times the speed of sound at 90,000 feet and fly coast to coast without refueling. The highly skilled Technical Design and Engineering Division of Lockheed Skunk Works under the leadership of Kelly Johnson was once again called upon to develop a replacement aircraft. These engineers went to work and the outcome of their design efforts produced an extraordinary plane, the CIA A-12 Oxcart.

Although officially replaced by the A-12 Oxcart the U-2 continued to fly reconnaissance missions in addition to weather surveillance, high altitude research, measuring radiation levels, and tracking and recovery of space capsules. The U-2 is one of a limited number of military planes to serve for over sixty years. Since 1994, some two-billion dollars has been invested to modernize the U-2 airframe and sensors, and re-engineer the program. The last variant of this legendary aircraft, the U-2S, is still in service and it remains one of the best intelligence platforms among those operated by the US Air Force. In early 2015, the Air Force was directed to restart modest funding for U-2 operations, research, development, and procurement through to fiscal year 2018. The RQ-4 was scheduled to replace the U-2 by 2019, but Lockheed claims the U-2 can remain viable until 2050.

Through patriotism, creativity, and willingness to take on the difficult CL-282 U-2 project, these aviation pioneers were committed to success. Irrespective of the adversities they faced, this group of Lockheed engineers, technicians, pilots and support personnel did what they set out to do, not for money, possessions or fame, but to help protect and preserve the security of the United States. What they were willing to sacrifice to be successful in advancing the quality and quantity of military intelligence is admirable. They played a crucial part in winning the Cold War by providing the opportunity for the US to look behind the Iron Curtain to "seek the truth" and gain an unequaled intelligence gathering advantage over the Soviet Union.

On 25 April 1962, the A-12 Oxcart supersonic spy plane become a reality.

MRBM LAUNCH SITE 2
SAN CRISTOBAL
1 NOVEMBER 1962

FUEL TRAILERS

MISSILE-READY TENT

FORMER LAUNCH POSITIONS

FORMER LOCATION OF MISSILE-READY TENTS

One of the first reconnaissance images of missile sites under construction in Cuba.
(Courtesy US Air Force and the CIA)

The U-2 Statistical Data
As Published by Wikipedia & Encyclopedia Britannica

Manufacturer: Lockheed Aircraft Corp.
Number of planes produced: 104
Crew: 1
Length: 63 ft 0 in
Height: 16 ft 0 in
Wingspan: 105 ft
Air Frame Material: Aluminum
Gross Takeoff Weight: 40,000 lb
Power Plants: Early versions had a Pratt & Whitney J75 turbojet engine, while later versions were powered by a General Electric F118-101turbofan engine, 17,000 lbf thrust

Fuel Capacity: 2,950 US gal
Range: 6,090 nautical miles
Cruise Speed: Mach 0.715
Maximum Speed: 410 mph
Climb Rate: 9,000 ft/min
Service Ceiling: 80,000 ft
Fuel Consumption: 910 lb/h in cruise
Cost: $950,000 per plane in 1955
Last U-2 Flight: Continues in operation today

A U-2 landing at Beale AFB. Note the bicycle wheel landing configuration.
(Courtesy US Air Force)

A U-2 attempts a carrier landing under Project Whale Tale.
(Courtesy CIA)

14

CIA A-12 SUPERSONIC SPY PLANE

The Second Specially Designed Spy Plane.
(Courtesy US Air Force Defense Visual Information Center)

The A-12 supersonic spy plane was the replacement for the U-2, and a pioneering achievement in aeronautical engineering. The initial concept for the new spy plane was to operate at stratospheric altitudes and therefore required new design, construction, and materials However, the most pressing question was what metal could be used in these most demanding flight conditions? The traditional aircraft metal, aluminum, turned to jelly at Mach 2.6, and was therefore rendered unusable for this new plane designed to cruse at Mach 3. Any other metal or alloy in current use had its own deficiencies and was also unusable, posing a major problem for these avionic design engineers.

After months of research and testing, a newly invented titanium alloy was deemed the best metal to use because; its hardness would withstand the advanced temperatures produced during high altitude flying at supersonic speed, and it was resistant to corrosion. Perhaps the most important feature for the A-12 was it had the highest strength-to-weight ratio of any metal, which meant titanium was approximately 45% lighter than steel. There was just one little problem. The US had a very limited supply of this titanium alloy. On the other hand, the Soviet Union possessed an abundant supply. But how could the US get enough titanium to build an aircraft? The proposed solution was to create dozens of shell US companies and use them to buy enough titanium supplies from the Soviets to produce the plane. The US was successful in this devious plot and the new strategic reconnaissance aircraft was manufactured. It is ironic that the Soviets unknowingly supplied the titanium to build the airplanes which would subsequently fly over their country and spy on their activities.

However, as would be discovered later, the rigid quality of titanium also created a monumental problem for cutting, machining and shaping. Even basic drill bits which worked well on aluminum and other aircraft metals broke with minimum use. If this new alloy was to be used, new ways to fabricate it and new tools were needed. During the development process, the team also discovered that titanium was highly sensitive to chlorine. Bolts which had been welded began to fail after only six weeks of use. After some investigating it was determined that the Burbank public water used to rinse the welds contained a significant amount of chlorine. Solution: use distilled water and problem solved.

The first version of the new CIA spy plane was a one-seat plane called the A-12 Oxcart. The "A" represented Lockheed's internal aircraft code name "Archangel," the number "12" designated it the twelfth in a series of internal designs, and "Oxcart" was the CIA selected project code name. Former US Army cartographer and retired Professor of Geography Gary M. Green makes the observation that ironically, in northwest Russia, where the Northern Dvina River empties into the White Sea, is the city of Arkhangelsk, translated "Archangel" in English. A name derived from the Michael Archangel Monastery located there. In the 1400s, Arkhangelsk was important in the rivalry between Norwegian and Russian interests in the northern areas. During both World Wars, Archangel was a major port of entry for allied aid, providing supplies to Russian troops cut off from normal supply lines. So, we have a spy plane code named Archangel, made from Russian titanium alloy, created by the CIA to fly spy missions over the Russian mother land. Isn't that interesting?

However, according to the *Roadrunners Internationale* website, no self-respecting pilot wanted to fly anything named "Oxcart." The first visual image was a wooden wagon pulled by a slow, dim-witted ox, lumbering along the street, and certainly not a proper name for a super-fast spy plane. So, Lockheed unofficially dubbed them "Cygnus" after the constellation, the Swan. That wasn't the best name, but certainly an improvement over "Oxcart."

15

A-12 FINAL TESTING
AND DUTY ASSIGNMENT

As with the U-2, the A-12 could not be tested at the Palmdale plant for obvious reasons. The plane had to be moved to Area 51 for testing. Obviously, the CIA could not risk flying the A-12 from the Palmdale plant to the Area 51, and unfortunately, because of its size it could not be transported by cargo plane as was the U-2. That left transporting overland by truck. The first trip was made in February 1962, with three additional trips in 1962 and 1964, for the remaining A-12s. More detail is included in Chapter 11, Experimental Aircraft Testing Area 51.

The team incurred a plethora of technical problems during developmental testing some of which seemed to be almost unsurmountable. For example, the spike's hydraulic control units which regulated the air flow into the engine would not respond quickly enough to manage the supersonic air flow, resulting in engine failure. It took almost a year to correct this problem. As 1964 ended, the eleven planes at Area 51 had logged some 1200 test flights and 1700 flying hours, but only thirty-three minutes at Mach 3.2, the expected cruise speed. Finally, an air-inlet control system solution was developed and on 27 January 1965, an A-12 flew for one hour and fifteen minutes at a speed of Mach 3. The air flow problem appeared to be solved.

These pilots and engineers wrote the operations manual as the results of each test flight were evaluated. Changes were made systematically and flight procedures revised and updated during debriefings. By November 1965 the final validation flights for deployment were finished. During these tests, the A-12 achieved a maximum speed of Mach 3.29, (2504 mph), a flight level of 90,000 feet, with a sustained flight time above Mach 3.2 of seventy-four minutes, an unbelievable accomplishment. Kelly

Johnson once made the statement that "The idea of attaining and staying at Mach 3.2 over long flights was the toughest job the Skunk Works® ever had and the most difficult of my career." After several delays, partly because of political concerns and accidents, the A-12 Oxcart was finally declared mission ready.

Unfortunately, successfully fulfilling its primary objective of replacing the U-2 in flights over the Soviet Union and Cuba had become doubtful. In fact, it was never used for either surveillance role. Advancements in the Soviet air defense system made even an aircraft flying at these higher altitudes and faster speeds detectable and trackable, and the US knew the Soviets continued to work on SAM modifications to reach these altitudes, increasing the A-12 vulnerability to an unacceptable level.

Replacing the Soviet Union and Cuba was the new target, Vietnam, and the Operations location was Kadena Air Base, Okinawa, Japan. Kadena has been occupied by the US since 1945 when it was seized from the Japanese during WWII, and has functioned as a strategic Theater of Operation (OL-8) for the A-12s and eventually the SR-71A. The declassified CIA document relating to the Oxcart Operations Plan on page 114 authorizes three planes and support staff to be deployed to Kadena Air Base under an operation titled Black Shield. Those three A-12 planes were numbers 930, 932 and 937, with the first plane arriving 22 May 1967.

The CIA would be responsible for planning, directing and controlling each operational mission from OL-8. With agreeable weather, the anticipation was that the Oxcart could fly nine successful missions per month and additional proficiency sorties as needed. To accommodate any developing emergency situation or weather problems, missions were on a twenty-four-hour alert status for each launch. Ensuring the operational readiness of the required number of aircraft at any given time, the directive required planes to be used on a rotation basis to provide adequate time for repair and maintenance.

As with the U-2 program, a special pre-flight process was necessary. Two hours prior to launch, the pilot was transported to the Physiological Support Division (PSD) building and given a medical examination. If the pilot was cleared for flying, with the assistance of the PSD Technicians, he put on his pressure suit, transferred to a portable oxygen container and transported to the plane. Again, a more comprehensive discussion of the PSD process is included in Chapter 26, Getting Suited-Up.

II. OXCART RECONNAISSANCE OPERATIONS PLAN

1. The required photographic coverage of North Vietnam will be accomplished by the OXCART vehicle operating from Kadena Air Base in Okinawa. This operating location at Kadena has been prepared for OXCART operation for some time.

2. Operational missions will be planned, directed and controlled by the Central Intelligence Agency Operations Center. Three OXCART aircraft and the necessary task force personnel will be deployed from Area 51 to Kadena.

3. With this inventory a minimum of nine (9) successful operational missions per month can be flown consistent with available weather. Overcast skies are a predominate feature associated with the monsoon season and limit the number of days suitable for effective photographic reconnaissance. As the monsoon season wanes, the number of clear days increases permitting more frequent, repetitive reconnaissance coverage. Missions will be launched on a twenty-four hour alert basis. This will permit maximum utilization of the favorable weather available. In addition to the operational missions flown, necessary test and proficiency sorties will be flown from Kadena. OXCART aircraft will be rotated   to maintain the required number of operationally ready aircraft at Kadena.

(Courtesy CIA)

16

PUBLIC ACKNOWLEDGEMENT
OF THE SECRET PLANE

The A-12 was a Top-Secret program as would be expected. There was no indication the Soviets knew anything about the dummy businesses used to secure the titanium, or that the US had even replaced the U-2 plane. For all practical purposes, the A-12 did not exist. Unfortunately, that secrecy created the illusion that the US was doing very little to keep up with the Soviets. From a military or political viewpoint, and especially during those Cold War years, that was not a good perception.

The Soviet space program appeared to be far advanced compared to the US space program. They launched the first satellite, Sputnik I, and in October 1957, Sputnik II launched carrying a dog named Laika, the first living creature to orbit the earth. The Soviets also sent the first human, Cosmonaut Yuri Gagarin, into space and earth orbit on Vostok I on April 12, 1961. All this was well in advance of Astronaut John Glenn's famous ride to orbit the earth on 20 February 1962 in Friendship 7.

Avoiding publicity, the U-2 caped in secrecy, continued to make regular reconnaissance flights over the USSR undetected and non-publicized. Additionally, another threat much closer to home, made reconnaissance missions even more important. In 1962, the Premier of the Soviet Union, Nikita Khrushchev and the Prime Minister of Cuba, Fidel Castro, consummated an agreement permitting the Soviets to install nuclear-capable ballistic missiles in Cuba, just ninety miles from the southern tip of Florida. That meant increased reconnaissance missions during the crisis, a naval blockade imposed by the US, and verification of the removal of the missiles. As referenced in Chapter 13, in October 1962 Major Rudolf Anderson Jr.'s U-2 was shot down by a SA-2 missile during the Cuban Missile Crisis. Until the U-2 was shot down, neither the Russians nor Cubans knew the A-12 was also flying reconnaissance missions over Cuba.

As designed, the A-12 program was so secret the general public and many who served in the Air Force were not aware of it, and many pilots heard only rumors of the program. Although the CIA and the Air Force were reasonably successful in this covert program, the crash of the first A-12 on 24 May 1963 lifted that cloak of secrecy. Newspaper reporters were not convinced by the Air Force's story that the plane was a F-105 was truthful, and news articles soon appeared. The Las Vegas Sun published an article with the headline, "Secret of sizzling new plane probably history's best kept secret." Even aviation enthusiasts soon picked up on the project often through sheer guesswork, according to the CIA's recently declassified official history.

During the 1963 campaign, Republican presidential nominee Barry Goldwater was relentless in his criticism of President Lyndon B. Johnson and his administration for falling behind the Soviet Union in the space program, and the research and development of new weapons systems. Despite these accusations, President Johnson successfully held on for a second term, but decided to counter this growing criticism by Mr. Goldwater and the press by releasing information on the highly classified spy program, and the existence of a new reconnaissance plane. On 29 February 1964, President Johnson announced that an A-11, a deliberate incorrect reference, had flown at sustained speeds of over 2000 mph at 70,000 feet during tests at Edwards AFB, CA. He said, "The existence of this program is being disclosed today to permit the orderly exploitation of this advanced technology in our military and commercial program." This announcement bolstered his campaign statements by contradicting the accusations made by Mr. Goldwater, but by doing so, the top-secret spy plane was no longer a secret.

On 24 July 1964, President Johnson announced the SR-71A development. The plane was originally designated RS-71, RS for Reconnaissance Strike and 71 to follow the RS-70 Valkyrie plane. However, Air Force Chief of Staff General Curtis LeMay preferred the Strategic Reconnaissance (SR) designation to the Reconnaissance Strike (RS), and lobbied to make the change. The President reluctantly agreed. Unfortunately, in preparing the White House press release, the change from "RS" to "SR" was never made. The news transcript provided to the press still had the earlier RS designation creating a story in the media that the president had misread the aircraft's designation. Even with the mistake, the designation stuck and SR-71A was the new official name. This simple designation variation forced designers into a monumental job of changing the name on some 33,000 different plane drawings and specification sheets, all by hand.

This public disclosure of the A-12 and the SR-71A Blackbird program came as a shock to everyone at the Lockheed Martin Skunk Works, the CIA, and Air Force personnel involved in the program. Much to their dismay, their highly classified secret was out, and the world knew. Now that the Soviets were aware of this new spy plane, protecting the Blackbird became a high priority. This would become the responsibility of the USAF Military Police, and increased security measures.

17

END OF THE ROAD FOR THE OXCART

A total of fifteen A-12 aircraft were built from 1962 to 1968, formally establishing the Oxcart family. Thirteen A-12s were mission operational, two were converted into a two-seat drone carrying plane and designated the M-21. Only one A-12 #06927 was built with a tandem seat used for training purposes. This trainer retired with 614 individual training flights and 1076.4 hours. It is on display outside the California Science Center in Los Angeles in the Roy A. Anderson Blackbird Exhibit & Garden.

The A-12 Oxcart began its operational missions with its deployment to Kadena, flying a total of twenty-two missions over North Vietnam during 1967. CIA Pilot Mele Vojvodich Jr. flew the first Black Shield mission over North Vietnam on 31 May 1967 at 80,000 ft and Mach 3.1 photographing surface-to-air missile sites. Additionally, these A-12 pilots flew sorties over China, North Korea and Cuba. The 29th and final A-12 mission was flown by CIA pilot Ronald L. Layton on 8 May 1968, over North Korea.

Although the A-12 represented a pioneering achievement in aeronautical engineering, it continued to be plagued with numerous technical problems. Engineers attempted to correct these problems, but the A-12 did not appear destined for sustained use. Additionally, the flight and reconnaissance multi-tasking work expected to be performed by a single pilot became a daunting task. Flying the plane at supersonic speed, monitoring all the controls, engaging the cameras, working the radio and keeping a watchful eye for danger was a task saturation condition. Assimilating, processing and reacting to all this information required more brain functionality and physical work than one person could effectively perform. Lockheed engineers knew all too well that as task saturation increased, performance decreased, and the potential for mistakes escalated. If this plane was to continue its reconnaissance work, another redesign was required.

Once again, the Technical Design and Engineering Division of Lockheed Martin Skunk Works' returned to the drawing board and using the A-12s principal design, developed another plane, the SR-71A Blackbird. Despite the problems and deficiencies of the A-12, its overall performance was remarkable and its success was amplified in the SR-71A Blackbird. How important was the A-12, you ask? Colonel Ken "Dutch 21" Collins (Ret.) sums it up in this statement, "If it hadn't been for the A-12, there wouldn't be an SR-71A."

Pilot Frank Murray made the final A-12 flight on 21 June 1968 to the storage facility at Palmdale, California. All surviving aircraft were transferred to and remained at the Palmdale facility for nearly twenty years before being sent to museums around the US. We are privileged to have three A-12s on display in Alabama-A-12 tail number 60-6930 is on display at the US Space & Rocket Center in Huntsville, A-12 tail number 60-6937 at the Southern Museum of Flight in Birmingham, and A-12 tail number 60-6938 is displayed at the Battleship Memorial Park in Mobile.

President Johnson ordered the retirement of the A-12s, and the program officially ended. As the transition process began to the SR-71A Blackbird, a comprehensive study was undertaken by the CIA to identify phase in options for the conversion of the A-12 to the SR-71A. A copy of "Option A" from that declassified CIA report to the Director, CIA Reconnaissance Programs dated 3 January 1968 is included on page 113.

When the SR-71A Blackbird rolled out, the next chapter in aerial reconnaissance had begun.

Option "A" of the CIA SR-71A Phase-in Process

TOP SECRET

Central Intelligence Agency
Attachment I To

OPTION A: UPDATE OF CURRENT PLAN FOR PHASE-IN OF THE SR-71A with NO OVERLAP WITH THE A-12.

1. The Ground Support Equipment, Test and Shop Equipment that is to remain in place for SR-71 support has already been identified and tagged. Supply spares and hardware also tagged. Items to be returned to [   ] after re—deployment have been identified.

2. SAC has already surveyed assets at Kadena for SR-71 operations permitting facile transition from OXCART to SR-71 operation.

3. Housing now used by OXCART will be available for SR-71 personnel based on scheduled OXCART withdrawal.

4. Kadena Air Base support now geared to accept influx of SR-71 program per previously co—ordinated plan.

5. No additional major construction required. SR-71 would use current OXCART facilities.

6. Orderly OXCART re—deployment and SR-71 deployment plan with necessary supporting plans are published and being kept current.

7. No problems from a security standpoint which have not been previously considered and for which provisions have been made.

8. Possibility exists of intelligence collection gap between Dates of OXCART operational cessation and actual reconnaissance Operation date of SR-71A.

25X1

TOP SECRET

25X1

Option "A" of the CIA SR-71A Phase-in Process.
(Courtesy CIA)

The A-12 Oxcart Statistical Data
As published by Wikipedia Encyclopedia

Manufacturer: Lockheed Aircraft Corp.
Number of planes produced-15
Crew: 1
Length: 101 ft 7 in
Height: 18 ft 6 in
Wingspan: 55 ft 7 in
Gross Takeoff Weight: 122,000 lb
Maximum Landing Weight: 52,000 lb
Power Plants: Two Pratt and Whitney JT11D-20B (J58-1) afterburning turbojet/ramjet, 20,500lbf dry thrust, producing up to 32,500 pounds of thrust with afterburners

Fuel Capacity: 10,590 US gal JP-7
Range: 2,500 nautical miles
Cruise Speed: Mach 3.2
Maximum Speed: Mach 3.35
Climb Rate: 11,800 ft/min
Service Ceiling: 85,000-90,000 ft
Cost: $16 million per plane
Missions: 29
Last A-12 Flight: 8 May 1968 over North Korea, pilot Ronald L. Layton.

A-12 (60-6924) takes off from Groom Lake on its maiden flight, 30 April 1962.
(Courtesy CIA)

NASA A-12 in Flight.
(Courtesy NASA)

18

YF-12A EXPERIMENTAL FIGHTER-INTERCEPTOR

(Courtesy CIA)

In the late 1950s, the US Air Force needed to replace its F-106 Delta Dart interceptor. Kelly Johnson, head of Lockheed Skunk Works®, proposed to build a version of the A-12 designated as YF-12A interceptor for the USAF. The first YF-12A flew on 7 August 1963, and one of its Air Force test pilots, James Benson "Jim" Irwin, would become a NASA astronaut and walk on the Moon during the 1971 Apollo 15 mission. The YF-12A was a twin-seat version of the single-seat A-12, and a prototype contributing to the development of the twin-seat reconnaissance SR-71A. The YF-12A set a speed record of over 2,000 miles per hour, and an altitude world record of over 80,000 feet which were later surpassed by the SR-71A. The YF-12A program was abandoned following the cancellation of the production in 1968. Of the three YF-12As built, number 60-6934 was damaged beyond repair by fire during a landing mishap on 14 August 1966 at Edwards AFB, and YF-12A number 60-6936 was lost on 24 June 1971 because of an in-flight fire caused by a failed fuel line. YF-12A number 60-6935 is the only survivor and it is on display at the National Museum of the United States Air Force at Wright-Patterson Air Force Base near Dayton, Ohio

19

THE SR-71A SUPERCHARGED AND SUPERSONIC

The Last Specially Designed Spy Plane.
(Courtesy NASA EC 95-43075)

The U-2 and A-12 Oxcart aircraft played a meaningful role in Cold War reconnaissance, but unfortunately the effective service life for both planes was short. The engineers and technicians used the data acquired from both of these aircraft to develop a spy plane which became the crown jewel of US aerial reconnaissance, the SR-71A Blackbird. In many ways the Blackbird was unbelievable, unstoppable, and for reconnaissance purposes, almost unlimited. The sophisticated Blackbird has been described as more of an engineering marvel requiring an "Avionics Engineer" to fly it. There was a series of thirty-two planes manufactured: twenty-nine SR-71As, two SR-71AB trainers, one SR-71AC, a hybrid aircraft developed at the end of the program. For simplicity and journalistic purposes, the generic term SR-71, or Blackbird, is often used in this book.

Twelve SR-71As were "lost to accidents" between 1966 and 1972, killing one pilot, but no plane was lost to, or damaged by, enemy action. It is the only US plane to hold that distinction. The first SR-71A test flight was conducted on 22 December 1964, and the final flight was 9 October 1999 with 3,551 mission sorties and a combined total of 53,490 hours of flight time between those dates. The SR-71A has been given several unofficial nicknames over time, including: Sled, Lady in Black, and Habu, but the name most recognized is "the Blackbird."

Under a new program combining the CIA A-12 Oxcart and USAF SR-71A, code named "Senior Crown," Lockheed Martin's engineers and technicians developed a variation of the A-12 with two cockpits: one for a pilot and one for a Reconnaissance Systems Officer (RSO). With a bulkhead separating them, they communicated via the plane's intercom system. This new plane was about six feet longer than the A-12 Oxcart and weighed an additional 15,000 pounds when fully loaded.

New reconnaissance equipment including signal intelligence sensors, side-looking radar and six updated photo cameras were added. As standard equipment, the re-designed Blackbird carried a Fairchild Terrain Objective Camera and initially, an HRB Singer infrared tracking camera. Both cameras ran during the entire mission for reconnaissance photos and route documentation to respond to any accusations of inappropriate flight pattern allegations. One reason the Blackbird produced such highly detailed photographs with such great clarity was because it had an excellent autopilot. Not only was it the primary method to control the aircraft, it was the most stable platform from which to operate the cameras and imaging sensors. The autopilot was so sensitive it could control the speed to 1/100 of a Mach.

The 1960s were not a time of great aerial technological advancement. Planes were designed with conventional flight control round analog gauges with few, if any, digital displays. Even the Blackbird had only one triple digital display instrument which gave the air data computer information (e.g., knots equivalent airspeed), the altitude, and the Mach number. All other displays were the same as in fighter planes. There was no "Star Wars" technology in this plane but interestingly, the extremely accurate sixty-one star tracking celestial navigation system was nicknamed "R2 D2," after an astromech droid creation by Akira Kurosawa's for his 1958 movie, *The Hidden Fortress*, and made popular in the movie Star Wars. ®

The plane was extensively tested and approved for use officially replacing the CIA's U-2 and A-12 aircraft. It is reported that on the first test flight, 22 December 1964, there were 383 unresolved items remaining on the plane's final completion checklist. Knowing that, I wonder what test pilot Robert J. "Bob" Gilliland was thinking as he took off on that first test flight? Experiencing no significant problems, Bob attained a Mach 1.5 speed at an altitude of 50,000 feet that first time out, as corrections, modifications and adjustments. continued to be made.

After the Blackbird was operational, the next big consideration was where to assign responsibility for the plane. The aircraft had no armament, so fighter groups felt no kinship. It couldn't drop bombs, so the bomber groups had little use for it. From either group's perspective, it would be an unwarranted expense item in a budget conscious environment. After much debate the Department of Defense (DOD) decided to fund the program through the USAF Strategic Air Command (SAC), and Palmdale AFB, California would be home for the new Blackbird. This seemed like an awkward paring since SAC's primary mission was supporting bombers. Records indicate that SAC didn't see the Blackbird contributing to its mission objectives and didn't want the plane under its command. That said, the Blackbird remained as assigned by the DOD. The 4200th Strategic Reconnaissance Wing was activated at Beale AFB on 1 January 1965, and the first SR-71A, number 61-7958, was delivered on 24 May 1966. The wing designation was changed to the 9th Strategic Reconnaissance Wing on 25 June 1966 and remains so designated today.

Once activated, the Blackbird became the premier reconnaissance plane monitoring Soviet nuclear submarine, mobile missile site and troop movements on a weekly schedule. It also continued its surveillance flights over North Vietnam, Red China, North Korea, the Middle East, Cuba, Nicaragua, Iran, Libya, the Falkland Islands, and other countries until it was officially retired in 1999.

In March 1968 a detachment of Blackbirds was transferred to Kadena in an operation called "Glowing Heat." Upon arrival, the native people saw this strange and dangerous looking plane and likened it to a poisonous pit viper they called a "Habu." The name stuck and soon SR-71A air crews were referred to as Habus. Crew members who flew operational sorties proudly wore a specially designed arm patch on their uniform designating them as Habus.

The first USAF/SAC SR-71A number 61-976 operational flight launched on 21 March 1968 over North Vietnam, with pilot Major Jerry O' Malley and RSO Captain Edward Payne at the controls. This aircraft accumulated 2,981 flying hours and flew a total of 942 sorties, more than any other SR-71A in the fleet. Since March 1990 it has been on display at the National Museum of the United States Air Force near Dayton, OH. For twenty-two years, this Kadena Air Base Blackbird detachment flew a total of 2,410 missions over Vietnam, Laos, Cambodia, North Korea, and South China. Fortunately, very few people knew of the existence of the Blackbird, or the significant role it played through its surveillance. Shrouded in secrecy, the Blackbird secured information on activities which could pose a threat to the US or one of our allies.

The plane's nickname Blackbird was derived from the special dark paint on its exterior, which helped to maintain its stealth mode. Prior to each mission, a crew of paint specialists ensured there were no imperfections in the skin that would compromise its stealth characteristics. Over sixty pounds of black paint was used to cover each plane. Special elements in the dark paint also aided in counteracting the high temperatures incurred during a supersonic flight. For example, at Mach 3 (2283.6 mph) the leading edges of the plane could reach 876 degrees Fahrenheit, while the rest of the plane's skin was a cool 500 degrees Fahrenheit.

The fifty-five-foot-long wings were constructed with ridged surfaces to avoid cracks or buckling caused by differential heat expansion. The airframe parts were also made to fit loosely while the plane was on the ground, and expanded and fit more snugly when exposed to high temperatures during flight.

Because of the U-2's vulnerability at 68,000 to 70,000 feet, the Blackbird was designed to reach 90,000 to 100,000 feet if necessary. However, the Blackbird generally operated between 70,000 and 80,000 feet. To provide a perspective of that altitude, the stratosphere, the second major layer of Earth's atmosphere, starts at 23,000 to 53,000 feet, varying with latitude and seasons, and extends to 160,000 feet. Since the aircraft has no munitions systems, its only defense was the ability to fly high and fast. Each of the Blackbird's twin Pratt & Whitney J58 jet engines was capable of 32,500 pounds of static thrust giving it the capability of flying at speeds of more than sustained Mach 3+ (2,200 miles per hour, or more than three times the speed of sound).

The Blackbird's highly sophisticated spy equipment permitted it to survey and record on film 100,000 square miles of the Earth's surface per hour from an altitude of 80,000 feet. The Technical Objective Camera (TEOC) lens was developed in 1960 by the ITEK Corporation with the capability to take a clear photographic image of a six-inch object on the ground while operating at an altitude of 85,000 feet. In one website article, an RSO boasted, "it can read the numbers on your car tag while flying Mach 3 at 80,000." Another pilot was a bit more definitive saying, "the camera had the ability to read the numbers on the odometer of a convertible traveling on the highway with the top down." That is an astonishing photographic capability. Because the aircraft was traveling some 3,000 feet per second, eliminating film distortion was paramount to producing a usable photograph sequence. The solution required technical innovations in both navigational control and photography. The TEOC had two shutter speeds, a slow speed of forty, and a high-speed of eighty inches per second. Therefore, the time needed to expose the slower shutter speed of forty for one nine-inch photographic frame was 0.225 of a second, and 0.1125 for the high-speed. A bit more complicated than aim, focus and click for our K-1 DSLR Pentax® camera. Although important, the camera's shutter speed wasn't the only consideration for clarity. The camera was only as good as the film used. For maximum image detail, the film had to be of a quality that produced high resolution, excellent contrast, and fine detail.

These high-resolution cameras required a stabilized temperature which posed another significant challenge since the exterior of the aircraft could reach 450 degrees in normal operation mode, and then decrease to a minus forty-five degrees temperature at a lower flight level. To maintain a stabilized temperature, the engineers devised a method to ensure cameras were cooled at the normal operating altitude and then reversed to heat them at lower altitudes, such as when refueling.

The Blackbird was not designed as an aggressor plane and had no way to defend itself other than speed and altitude. One website made the observation that the Blackbird's Missile Avoidance Technique was a "middle finger" to the would-be attackers. It could out fly and out maneuver any aircraft or missile in pursuit of it, provided the aircrew was aware of a SAM or an Air-to-Air (ATA) launch. The RSO monitored the Electronic Countermeasures (ECM) panel, providing the ability to determine whether or not the enemy was tracking them on radar, or had fired a missile. Research information indicates that numerous missiles, up to 4,000, were fired at the Blackbird during its service time, but none came close to contact. The prime directive of the Blackbird was to accomplish the reconnaissance mission, and these air crews were never deterred from that mission by any enemy threat.

The Soviet MiG-25 Foxbat was the only plane that came come close to the Blackbird's speed. The MiG-25, designed to function both as a long-range interceptor and reconnaissance aircraft, lacked technological refinement, but its capabilities and performance caused much concern. It could reach a Mach 2.8 speed but could sustain that speed for only a few minutes, because above Mach 2.8 the engines would overheat and burn up. In 1973, US Air Force Secretary Robert C. Seamans stated, "The MiG-25 was probably the best interceptor in production in the world today." Often, the Soviets sent a MiG-25 to chase the Blackbird to its maximum altitude and hope to get lucky firing an ATA missile. They tried diligently but were never successful hitting the Blackbird.

The *Daily Beast* posted a story about Viktor Belenko, a Soviet MiG-25 pilot, a defector to Japan in 1976, with a high regard for the SR-71 and its crew. He made this statement, "They [SR-71A crew] taunted and toyed with the MiG-25s sent up to intercept them, scooting up to altitudes the Soviet planes could not reach, and circling leisurely above them or dashing off at speeds the Russian planes could not match." Without a doubt, that frustrated these MiG pilots.

During its service life 1964 through 1999, not much was known about the Blackbird, and as a special plane flying covert missions, that is the way it should have been. The less information available, the better the chances of successful missions. There is an old proverb that says the devil's greatest triumph was getting people to believe he doesn't exist. Perhaps one reason for the SR-71 Blackbird's greatest triumphs was that for many years, very few people knew it existed.

20

THE TITANIUM GOOSE: SR-71B TRAINER

The SR-71B, a trainer aircraft with double pilot cockpits.
(Courtesy NASA EC 97-439021)

The SR-71AB was modified with a raised second cockpit and dual controls providing an instructor pilot the ability to train other pilots. Planes number 61-7956 and number 61-7957, were the two production "B" model SR-71As, and were operated by NASA's Dryden Flight Research Center at Edwards AFB, California from 1991-1997. Aircraft number 61-7956 logged a total of 3,967.5 flight hours, and its last flight was 19 October 1997 at the Edwards AFB Open House. It was placed on display at the Kalamazoo Aviation History Museum in Kalamazoo, MI. The second SR-71B, number 61-7957, crashed on approach to Beale AFB on 11 January 1968. Only one A-12 number 06927, nicknamed "Titanium Goose" was built, often referred to as the "A-12B" because of its SR-71B-like rear seat. This trainer retired with 614 individual training flights and 1076.4 hours. It is on display outside the California Science Center in Los Angeles in the Roy A. Anderson Blackbird Exhibit & Garden.

21

THE BASTARD: SR-71C

(Courtesy Hill Air Force Base)

After the crash of SR-71B 61-7957 in 1968, another trainer replacement aircraft was built. It was designated SR-71C, number 61-7981. It was the only "C" model Blackbird, and the last SR-71 to be manufactured. It was nicknamed "The Bastard" because it was a hybrid comprised of the rear fuselage of the first YF-12A (60-6934) and a functional engineering mockup of an SR-71A forward fuselage. The "C" model's first flight was 14 March 1969 from the Lockheed plant, Palmdale, California, with Blackbird

Chief Project Pilot Robert J. Gilliland at the controls and Lockheed test pilot Steve Belgeau as RSO. With flight testing completed, it was delivered to the 9th Strategic Reconnaissance Wing at Beale AFB, California, on 3 September 1970. Unfortunately, this aircraft never lived up to the usability of the SR-71A because of irregular maintenance procedures, and its aftermarket construction caused the aircraft to fly in a constant yaw. Consequently, the SR-71C was used on a limited basis from 1969-1976. The aircraft made its last flight on April 11, 1976 and was removed from flying status on June 24, 1976 with only 556.4 flight hours.

22

SECURITY FOR THE SPECIAL SPY PLANES

USAF Security Forces Shield

After General "Billy" Mitchell's success establishing the Air Force, one of the primary considerations was how to best use this new branch of service for the benefit of the US during the Cold War. Espionage activities between the Western Allies (US, UK and NATO) and the Eastern Bloc (the Soviet Union and countries aligned with the Warsaw Pact) were at their height during these years. Certain that another war was imminent, each side focused on ways to create an advantage over the other. As the US learned in WWII, information was a key component of winning. Securing good intelligence of the opposing side's intentions, military, and technology was paramount to success. Government spy agencies such as the CIA in the US and the KGB in the Soviet Union came into existence partly for the purpose of fulfilling the need to covertly gather intelligence. Once these agencies understood the value of using aircraft for easier, quicker and more expanded intelligence gathering, the planes we have discussed in this book became a reconnaissance reality.

Certainly, protecting these high-level reconnaissance assets such as the U-2 and the Blackbird from espionage or sabotage was a top priority. Because these aircraft were part of an Air Force program, protection responsibility was assigned to the Air Force Military Police. The heritage of this police group dates back to 1947 when the National Security Act created the USAF, and the "Military Police Company" was part of that creation. In 1948, the Military Police Company was realigned into the "USAF Air Police" and in an effort to more accurately reflect the security aspect of their mission, in 1966, it was subsequently re-named the "USAF Security Police Group." As the group transformed into more of a combat support force it was again re-formed and in 1997 it became the "USAF Security Forces" and remains so titled today.

Each Blackbird Operating Location had a security force squadron assigned to it. The 9th Security Police Squadron at Beale AFB, CA stood guard over the SR-71A Blackbirds for a period of twenty-five years and continue to protect the U-2 reconnaissance aircraft today. A few of the other locations included: the 18th Security Forces Squadron at Kadena AB, the 100th Security Forces Squadron at RAF Mildenhall, the 4th Security Forces Squadron at Seymour Johnson AFB, and the 6510th Air Police Squadron, Edwards AFB.

Some locations such as Beale AFB, provided a separate hangar for each plane. However, at other locations such as RAF Mildenhall, two planes were housed in one hangar. Access to restricted areas, or facilities, was prioritized based on the asset being protected, and access required verifiable authority and identity. Many high-level security resources included entry procedures enforced by an Entry Control Point (ECP) guard, often accomplished through a badge exchange. When an individual desired facility entry, he/she exchanged his/her restricted area badge at the ECP for a badge to be worn while inside the facility. This procedure was used by the CIA at Area 51 in 1955 when the U-2 testing started. The ECP guards had the responsibility to verify the individual's photograph and physical description on the badge prior to granting entry.

In an interview with Security Force Staff Sergeant (SSgt) Roy Price, he stated, "The hangars housing the Blackbird had an ECP controller for the facility, and a Close Boundary Sentry who guarded the restricted area boundaries. Additionally, several roving patrols with quick response capabilities were utilized during each shift. Equipped with M-16s while on the flight line guarding the Blackbird and a 38 or 9mm while on patrol duty, we provided protection twenty-four hours per day, seven days a week, prepared to confront any potential problem or issue."

In an article published in *Top Gun Bio*, David Baranek, a Navy Top Gun Instructor, related his first time to see a Blackbird which almost got him in trouble. He was conducting training at the Naval Air Station Key West in April 1986 at the same time an SR-71A was there due to an emergency landing. Curious to see this famous plane, David went to the hangar with his camera, never anticipating the camera would cause such a problem. Six security policemen bearing M-16 assault rifles immediately approached him advising that the hangar was a restricted access area and photography was not permitted. David assured them he had not taken any photos. One of the security policemen asked for David's identification card, took down his information and told him that should they see any photos of that plane in that hangar, they would be contacting him. I am certain David thought it was exciting to see the Blackbird, but even more exciting to leave the facility.

The Blackbird was so well guarded, I found no publicized incidence of an attempted espionage or sabotage effort. Then again, I am certain that information would be highly classified and therefore not available to the public. I inquired of SSgt. Roy Price about any incident he remembered and he replied, "None that I know of. However, my security clearance level would prevent me from being privileged to that type of information." I suspect because of the security force's work, there were few attempts, if any.

Flying the Blackbird

Because the Blackbird's design made it such a unique plane, the process of flying it was just as unique. The technical procedures, developed through the trial-and-error operations of the Blackbird's predecessors the U-2 and A-12, are captivating. These procedures were meticulously followed from the initial flight preparation to the final landing and return to the hangar. The details of flying the Blackbird in the following chapters will put you in the middle of an extraordinary process, and will fascinate you.

23

THE BLACKBIRD PILOT

Becoming a Blackbird pilot was a long process beginning with earning the silver wings of an Air Force pilot, and meeting the requirements of the USAF pilot training program was challenging to say the least. Undergraduate Pilot Training (UPT) Phase 1 involved four to six weeks of twelve-hour days attending classes learning about; aircraft systems, flight regulations, instrument flying, aerospace physiology, navigation, flight planning, and aviation weather, in addition to computer based training, and physical exercise. Pilot training was a high intensity environment with no promise of success. It made no difference what university you attended, where you came from or how chummy your family was with politicians, UPT was an equal-opportunity endeavor. Either you made it on your own, or you didn't.

Following successful completion of the UPT Phase 1 training, trainees began Phase 2, the advanced flight phase of simulator and aircraft training. One trainee remarked, "I was so excited to finally be in the flying phase." It is estimated that the Air Force spends some six million dollars to train and ready the pilot for combat.

After graduating pilot training school and being assigned to a fighter, bomber or support squadron, most every pilot is given a call sign. This sign is used to identify the individual aircrew members during flights without using names or rank designations, and usually represents something distinctive about the pilot. Often squadron mates select the call sign and the pilot gets no input in the selection and definitely no power of change, only disapproval. Every pilot should be fortunate enough to receive a cool call sign like Viper, Hammer, Malibu, Superman, Cowboy or Maverick, but that's not always the case. Unfortunately, many call signs tend to come as a result of something embarrassing or perhaps humorous that a pilot did. Gabby, Moose, Wrong Way, or Stinky are just a few suitable for printing. Retired Blackbird Pilot Lt. Col. Ed Yeilding told me his call sign was "Dagger," but didn't elaborate on how he acquired it, and I didn't ask.

In a telephone conversation with USAF former U-2 pilot Major Greg Kimbrough, he told me he was flying his jet through French air space on a diplomatic flight plan conversing with a French Air Traffic Controller who was attempting to make a change in his flight plan. "Because of his broken English and rapid speech, it was difficult to understand him. Several times I asked him to slow down and repeat his instructions. I could tell the controller was becoming agitated with me, perhaps thinking I was toying with him. 'Where are you from with such a heavy country accent?' the controller asked me. Proud to say the state of Alabama in the USA, I responded. My fellow Air Force pilots monitoring my conversation with the controller got quite a laugh out of my situation. At the officer's club that evening, they kidded me profusely and dubbed me "'Kuntry" as my call sign, and it stuck, and I was Kuntry until I retired."

The call sign process was different in the SR program. Instead of using individual call signs to identify pilots and RSOs, a uniform identification name and mission number was used. For example, "Aspen" was used as the identification name at Kadena AB. Thus, a Blackbird mission could have been designated as Aspen 1150. Once airborne, refueled, and given the clearance to climb to its operational altitude, there was no contact with air traffic control or chatter between the Blackbird and any other plane, eliminating the need to use a call sign. When the Blackbird was inbound and reestablished air traffic control communications, it resumed the Aspen identification call sign. Retired Blackbird pilot Lt. Col. Dave Fruehauf said while he was at Edwards AFB, the standard identification was "Dutch" and the last three digits of the plane's tail number.

Research indicates the selection process for the Blackbird Strategic Reconnaissance Squadron (SRS) program was even more complicated than earning the pilot's silver wings. It was a very intense and methodical selection process, designed to choose the best people possessing the propensity to work together. The total number of pilots in this program was limited for several reasons. First, the limited number of SR-71A Blackbirds available to fly meant flying time would be reduced commensurately. Second, the SRS program was under command of the SAC, a bomber wing, and many fighter pilots considered this a downgrade in status. And third, just pilots who did not meet the physical, and psychological requirements.

In this volunteer program, the applicant assembled his qualifications including among other information; a personal biography, officer efficiency reports, performance and flight evaluations, flight time history, type aircraft flown, endorsements, and any recommendations. This information was submitted to the 9th Wing's Crew Selection Board for review. In a somewhat unusual procedure, the application process allowed existing SR-71A crews at Beale AFB to look over each applicant's file and make comments as to suitability for the program. This was a totally merit-based selection process, and politics played no part. In Fact, even attempting to use political connections or influence was detrimental. Ultimately it was a pilot's skills and disposition that qualified him into the program, not his politics.

Pilot candidates were required to be qualified in current high-performance fighters, emotionally stable, and sufficiently motivated for the program. Initially, the age range was between twenty-five and forty, and because of the size of the cockpit, physically under six feet tall and weigh less than 175 pounds. Each candidate was subjected to a rigorous physical examination. In fact, the physical exam was so extensive it often revealed physical problems that went undetected in the normal annual exam. The detection of a problem could disqualify the candidate not only from the Blackbird program, but in some cases, permanently ground the pilot from flying. This possibility alone became a determent to applying for the program for some pilots. In addition to the rigid physical exam, pilots interviewed with a psychiatrist and a psychologist. Each candidate was required to pass personal and professional evaluations involving interviewing his family. It was an intimidating process, and one filled with anxiety.

A high priority provision of the approval process was the security clearance. Because of the sensitive nature of the SR-71A program and the amount of highly classified information to which crew members were exposed, a clearance level greater than "top secret" was required. Every applicant had to meet the requirements for a Special Access Program (SAP) security clearance, a classification reserved only for highly sensitive military programs which is typical protocol for the military. Two things determined the level of security clearance required, the MOS/AFSC/Rating (occupation), and the specific job assignment. James Franklin, Chief

Engineer, Special Projects Office, Marshall Space Flight Center, explained this protocol. "A special background investigation was required to receive a top secret / SAP security clearance. However, even with this type security clearance, access to specific areas, buildings and information was granted on a 'need to know' basis, especially within a multi-faceted project." The Blackbird program operated under the same guidelines. No top secret/SAP security clearance, no Blackbird program approval.

If accepted, the applicant began a yearlong training program including many hours of classroom study and training time in the SR-71A simulator. The first two weeks consisted of classroom training on the aircraft including maintenance and repairs. Then, a pilot spent approximately three months in a simulator flying complicated training missions before being qualified to fly the Blackbird with a training pilot. After several training flights in the SR-71B with a training instructor and a successful solo flight, the pilot and RSO crew began to fly together.

There were no special Blackbird pilot wings to wear, but the distinctive orange color flight suit with the 1st Strategic Reconnaissance Squadron, the Mach 3+ and the Habu flight suit patches prominently displayed, distinguished them from other flying groups.

The Blackbird pilot and RSO positions were male dominated, and predominately white. Retired Col. Walter L. Watson, Jr was the exception. In 1984 he became the only African-American to qualify as an air crew member in the Blackbird program. Additionally, Col. Watson served as a flight instructor, and flight commander in tactical fighter and strategic reconnaissance squadrons. For his meritorious service, in 2004 Colonel Watson was awarded the *Brigadier General Noel F. Parrish Award,* the Tuskegee Airmen Inc.'s highest national award for service.

In October 1991, at the end of the Blackbird's active status, the first female was added to the program. Marta Bohn-Meyer, an aerospace engineer who had been at Dryden since 1979, was the first female crew member ever assigned to fly in the SR-71A, and one of only two flight engineers assigned to fly in the Dryden Research Center program at Edwards AFB. During these research flights she served as navigator and conducted research on aerodynamics, propulsion, thermal protection, and sonic booms which would be used in designing future aircraft. She and NASA test pilot Ed Schneider, were the last to fly the SR-71 at Mach 3.

1st Strategic Reconnaissance Squadron Wing, Beale AFB, California, 27 May 1967.
(Courtesy of Lieutenant Colonel Dave Fruehauf)

Left, SR-71A Pilot-Dave Fruehauf and RSO Gill Martinez, 1972.
(Courtesy of Lieutenant Colonel Dave Fruehauf)

24

PUSHING THE PEDALS
AND PULLING THE STICK

Going into the hanger housing the Blackbird was always a special time for any crew member. Just seeing this spectacular aircraft was always a thrill and being able to fly it was absolutely electrifying. In a March 2014 *SBNATION* interview with SR-71A pilot Captain Rick McCrary, Spencer Hall asked Rick about the first time he saw the plane, and Captain McCray responded, "We unlocked the back doors, turned on the lights, and I thought, Oh Lord, there's a spaceship." The Blackbird was a beautiful aircraft that always commanded attention whether on active duty or display. It was an aircraft certainly ahead of its time in terms of aviation technology in the 1960s. It had quite a performance record as indicated by the statistics following Chapter 34, and did I mention that pilots said it was an exciting aircraft to fly? Most, if not all, pilots had a feeling of exhilaration flying the Blackbird. Colonel Jim Wadkins, a USAF Blackbird pilot, put it this way, "At 85,000 feet and Mach 3, it was almost a religious experience. Nothing had prepared me to fly that fast. My God, even now I get goose bumps remembering."

With his superior intelligence and expectations for the future of flying, even English aerial engineer George Cayley could never have imagined his 1799 theories of weight, lift, drag and thrust would be used to develop an aircraft like the Blackbird.

As previously indicated, avionics equipment in the 1950s and 60s was primarily analog, although the high-tech Blackbird did have computerized navigation and photographic systems. As indicated in the photo on page 140, the SR-71 pilot cockpit instrument panel was a complex layout of instruments, gauges, displays, lights, toggles and switches, not including the many circuit breakers on the left and right arm panels. Retired Blackbird pilot Lt. Col. Dave Fruehauf said in our interview, "I flew the F4, F86, F100, and F101, but the SR-71 was the busiest cockpit I was ever in. It was a job keeping track of all the gauges, displays and instruments. The hands on some gauges turned clockwise, while others turned counter clockwise. Some indicators read from the bottom up while others read from the top down. Instrument cross-checking was certainly a challenge as your brain tried to determine if what you were seeing was good or bad. It was challenging to say the least."

Among all this highly technical equipment, one interesting device maintained in the cockpit was the "dingy stabber." What's a dingy stabber? Well, it was a piece of flat metal about six inches long with a point on one end used to puncture a life raft, should it accidentally inflate during flight. Not very high-tech, but without one, it would be a little difficult to control the plane flying Mach 3 with a cockpit filled with a life raft.

During flight, every pilot maintained a situational awareness mentality by continually cross-checking, and scanning all instruments for an indication of a malfunction of any type. In addition to flying the plane, the pilot also had to understand every system of the plane and constantly monitor the gauges for irregularity. Piloting the Blackbird commanded a more intense situational awareness, perhaps more than any other plane. As indicated in the photographs on page 141, the RSO had no flight control capability. He operated only the surveillance systems and navigational equipment from the rear cockpit during the mission. In the event of an emergency, the best the RSO could do was manipulate the navigational system to take the aircraft over friendly territory and then eject. I would suspect that flying at Mach 3, without flight control ability was not a pleasant thought for the RSO.

Most pilots agreed you could fly the Blackbird more proficiently if you had good stick and rudder skills. That simply means developing the ability to control an aircraft without total reliance on instruments and electronics. When pushing the pedals and pulling the stick, pilots cultivate sensitivity for the movements of the aircraft. They develop an appreciation for the plane's motion tolerance and that's the reason pilots like to fly the same aircraft mission after mission. Unfortunately, because of the limited number of Blackbirds and the number of scheduled missions, flying the same plane time after time was not possible. A pilot flew the plane available at the time.

Even with a pilot's manual flying proficiency, the Blackbird responded differently depending on how it was flying. Flying subsonic, below Mach 1, pilots compared it to flying the RF-4, very responsive to controls and changes. But at supersonic speed, above Mach 1, the Blackbird became less responsive and more difficult to control especially navigating a turn, thereby reducing any inclination to attempt manual flying, unless absolutely necessary.

Generally, there were only two planes at a detachment operating location, three tops. A pilot and RSO crew were assigned TDY (temporary duty) to an overseas base operation for a six-week deployment, and when completed, they returned stateside. After a crew was paired, they were seldom changed for a mission. The crew usually flew together or did not fly, creating the need for multiple crews at the base. Three crews were assigned to a base and they flew on a rotation basis. The first crew on the roster was primary, the second crew served as a backup in the event of a primary crew problem, and the third crew was on R&R (rest and relaxation).

SR-71A Pilot Cockpit.
(Courtesy US Air Force)

SR-71A Reconnaissance Systems Officer Cockpit.
(Courtesy US Air Force)

25

SR-71A PREFLIGHT PREPARATIONS

A tremendous amount of work was involved before any plane takes off, but pre-flight prep for a Blackbird was far more intense and detailed because of the special equipment required for each flight. As with all pre-flight checks, there was no room for error.

On the day prior to the mission, the Physiological Support Division (PSD) began the personal equipment evaluation process which included; the flight suit, helmet, gloves, the seat kit, parachute harness, communications connection, and ventilation hose. After each element was examined by a technician, the suit was fully assembled and pressurized to detect any potential problems. Any element indicating a discrepancy, or a "just doesn't feel right" to the technician was discarded without question. These elements would be inspected and evaluated at a later time but for this flight, they were not used. A two-technician cross-validation, dual-control system was used during the entire inspection and installation process. After all elements were approved for use, each element was logged into the pre-flight inspection sheet and retained together, for use on the following day's mission.

The ground crew began the pre-flight aircraft inspection check process eighteen to twenty-four hours prior to the mission. This was a labor intensive and lengthy process involving the usual complete exterior check, systems, instruments, tires, and lights in addition to the equipment specific to the Blackbird such as the drag chute, cameras, sensors, and the mission recording system. Cockpit control checks included; radio, ejection seat and canopy pins, circuit breakers, Triethylborane (TEB) counters, temperature indicators and several more.

Several hours were required to identify, ready and install the cameras and sensors used during a mission. An electronic computer tape was encoded with the automated pilot navigation instructions, and the camera's start and end commands which controlled the reconnaissance photography over the targeted areas. These were installed in the GAM-87 Astro-inertial Navigation System (ANS). Once the mission navigation and camera controls installation and plane checks were completed, the internal system check began, taking two hours or more. The PSD technicians checked among other things, all environmental controls and life support systems. After all these checks were made and verifications completed, the plane was confirmed mission ready. The Blackbird pilot and RSO put their full faith and trust in the work performed by the ground crew and PSD technicians.

First order of business for the pilot and RSO was the mission briefing with the operations officer, mission planners, weather and other personnel. At mission control, a flight plan was produced detailing the route to be flown, estimated time of arrival at specific points throughout the mission, and even the plane's designated banking angles for optimum photographic exposure. The briefing consisted of reviewing the mission plan's route, refueling points, expected weather conditions, navigation fix points, time over target and any identified threats it might encounter.

It was not unusual for the mission to be flown in a simulator the day prior to takeoff. In the USAF, the fighter pilot flight leader is trained to "chair fly" a mission by visualizing it in his or her head to see if it worked. Through this exercise, pilots often discovered an execution phase mistake and made changes before the mission began. The better the planning, the greater likelihood of mission success.

After attending the mission briefing, the pilot and RSO were ready for their pre-flight meal. Because most flights were lengthy, it was necessary to begin with a full stomach and adequately hydrated. A pre-flight meal consisted of a high protein, low residue meal of steak and eggs with coffee. A seasoned air crew knew not to eat anything highly combustible before the flight. "Any gastrointestinal problem within your pressure suit is most difficult to deal with at 70,000 feet," said one pilot. Intense concentration and flawless execution while being uncomfortable and given to flatulence was not the most desirable situation in which to be.

After the meal, the next order of business was to suit up for the flight.

26

GETTING SUITED-UP

After the briefing and meal, the Pilot and RSO were transported to the Physiological Support Division (PSD) building for their normal pre-flight preparations. The PSD unit was responsible for life support safety of the flight crew members. The first PSD was established 11 June 1957 when the US Air Force received the first six U-2s at Laughlin AFB, Texas, and the second PSD became operational 25 June 1966 when the first SR-71 Blackbirds arrived at Beale AFB, California.

The PSD unit was so diligent in its work, its commitment to pilots and RSOs who wore these suits was, once airborne, they will return safely, with or without the airplane. This commitment was tested and proven on 26 January 1966 when test pilot Bill Weaver developed an engine problem in his SR-71 number 64-17952. While the plane was disintegrating around them, Bill and the navigation systems specialist ejected from the plane at 78,800 while flying at Mach 3.18. "I didn't think the chances of surviving an ejection were very good," Bill states in a Chuck Yeager news article. The pressure suit and seat harness performed as designed, withstood extreme forces and provided a landing resulting in only a few bruises and a minor whiplash for Bill. Unfortunately, navigation systems specialist Jim Zwayer, suffered a broken neck during his ejection, which killed him instantly. Bill's safe landing in that New Mexico desert was positive proof of the PSD's dedication to life support for air crews. Because of their distinguished safety record, over the years, this exemplary PSD group received fifteen Air Force Outstanding Unit Awards and two Air Force Meritorious Unit Awards.

On the day of the flight, PSD launch and recovery technicians conducted a second pre-flight inspection of: the full pressure suit, communications system, oxygen system, parachute harness, water wings, seat kit and parachute ensuring they were in perfect working order.

To begin the pre-flight process, a PSD technician conducted a brief medical examination of each crew member checking; temperature, heart rate, and blood pressure. The PSD technician also inquired about the pilot and RSO's previous meals and sleep time, recording this information in the medical record book. Once approved for flight, it was time to suit up in their "Pilot Protective Assembly" golden S1030 full pressure flight suit.

Because of the physical impact of the high altitude and air speed, their fully pressurized flight suits were similar to those worn by the astronauts. In fact, my research indicated several of these suits were loaned to NASA to aid in perfecting space suits for their program. The flight suit used by the SR-71 crew members was a full body suit, gloves, and helmet, all connected together for pressurization purposes, and a seat harness connecting them to the plane. The purpose of the suit was to keep the crews alive under any situation inside or out of the airplane. Staff Sergeant (SSgt) Lola Wilson Fossett, a retired PSD Technician who was stationed at Beale AFB, told me in an interview, "Usually two PSD Technicians assisted each crew member in getting suited up. Because this was life support critical, it was a meticulous process involving a cross-check confirmation of every connection by each technician. Just knowing this person's life depends on how thoroughly you do your job is a sobering thought."

The body suit was a self-contained capsule of oxygen and controlled atmospheric pressure consisting of four layers: the nylon interior which provided some comfort next to the skin, the thermal layer which held the pressure for the suit, an outer mesh to aid in maintaining the shape of the suit when inflated, and the outer cover made of a flame and tear resistant material called Nomex. The suit had feet at the bottom of the legs, full-length sleeves with a locking metal ring used to connect the gloves, and a head opening with a locking metal ring to connect the helmet. Once these components were connected, the suit was pressurized and created a controlled environment. The suit could be worn non-pressurized provided the flight level was maintained below 50,000 feet.

As previously mentioned, the mission could extend to twelve hours. Consequently, after consuming liquids to remain hydrated during an extended flight, a crew member might develop the need to relieve himself. Defecating was not permitted, unless it was an absolute necessity, but urinating was anticipated. This function was accomplished through a Urine Collection Device (UCD) or a "piddle pack" as PSD technicians called it. As a first-generation Blackbird pilot, retired Lt. Col. Dave Fruehauf said his group was the first to successfully use the UCD after testing several other ineffective apparatuses. Lt. Col. Fruehauf said, "It took several tries and a few wet flight suits to get used to using the UCD, but we finally did, and on those ten to eleven-hour flights, it was appreciated."

With the assistance of a PSD technician, the crew member placed a soft rubber tube over his penis and secured it with tape. The tube was fitted through the nylon undergarment and secured to ensure the connection remained intact. This tube was attached to a UCD valve on a collection packet placed inside left thigh of the suit. The process was activated by adjusting the suit pressure regulator permitting the UCD valve to open and the airflow would allow urine to flow into the collection device and be absorbed by a sponge. At the conclusion, the UCD valve was closed by returning the suit pressure regulator back to its normal pressure, and the crew member giving a sigh of relief.

Although the UCD was available for use, the crew members used it less frequently than would be expected. First, most crew members limited the amount of liquid intake before a mission. Second, because the average mission lasted only five to six hours, it was not difficult to self-contain until landing. Third, the cool dry air within the pressure suit created an environment that contributed a loss of moisture through the skin. In one of our conversations, Retired Pilot Lt. Col. Ed Yeilding told me that during his 785 hours in the Blackbird, he used the UCD perhaps only two or three times, and in his book *SR-71A Revealed,* Pilot Col. Rich Graham said that in his 765 hours he never used it. However, knowing it was available was reassuring.

Once the UCD was in place and the undergarment was on, next came the body suit. Getting into the bulky suit was a cumbersome process requiring the assistance of two PSD technicians and about thirty to forty-five minutes. Pilots entered the body suit through a double zipper opening in the rear. While in a sitting position, the crew member put his legs into the suit first, then the arms into the sleeves and finally the head went through the "O" ring. The crew member then stood and the technicians zipped the suit together.

The specially fitted gloves were also of Nomex material with leather palms providing better grip, and were connected to the body suit sleeve by a metal ring locking the two together. Next came the harness, which was designed primarily for egress and survival. It consisted of the parachute harness with quick release fittings, rings attached to the seat straps on either side of the survival kit, and a flotation device in case the ejection occurred over water.

Physiological support equipment was not only designed to sustain aircrew members during flight, but also to provide environmental protection in any survival situation resulting from bailout, crash landing, or ditching. The unique missions of the U-2/SR-71A strategic reconnaissance aircraft required special equipment to provide maximum protection on a global basis. The list of items included in the "survival kit" was very extensive as indicated in Chapter Five of the Flying Operations U-2/SR-71A Physiological Support Equipment Requirements, Physiological Support Program, Air Combat Command Directive ACCI 11-459, Flying Operations U-2/SR-71, issued 10 MAY 96. Here's the list:

5.5. Mandatory Survival Kit Components and Quantity:

Life Raft/1 Each
AP/25S-5A/1 Each
Mark 13-MOD 0 or Mark 124/2 Each
Mirror, Signaling/1 Each
Sea Marker Dye/1 Each
Box, Waterproof w/Matches/1 Each
Kit, First Aid, Tropical (Box)/1 Each
Tourniquet/1 Each
Whistle, Plastic/1 Each
Survival Radio /PRC 90/112/1 Each
Spare Radio Battery/1 Each
Water, Drinking (Canned)/2 Each
Knife, Pocket/1 Each
Life Raft Repair Plugs/2 Each
Socks, Wool/1 Pair
Water Bag, Three Quarts/1 Each
Compass, Lensatic/1 Each
Desalter Kit/1 Each
Signaling Kit/1 Each
Strobe Light/1 Each

Strobe Light Filter/1 Each*
Mittens, Exposure/1 Pair
Rations, General Purpose/1 Each
Saw, Survival/1 Each
Sponge (camouflage)/2 Each
Wire Snare/20 Feet
Space Blanket/1 Each
Wool Ski Cap/1 Each
Goggles, Ski, Plastic/1 Pair
Survival Manual, AFM 64-5/1 Each
Survival Weapon, 9 mm/1 Each*
9mm Ammunition*
Light, Chemical/1 Each

*Equipment used at operating locations.

The GNS-1031 helmet was custom fitted for comfort and safety and included many technical components such as; a microphone adjusting knob, a dual oxygen regulator, a feeding port and the anti-suffocation device cover. A metal ring, located at the base of the helmet, locked into the neck ring of the body suit using spring-loaded latches. Combined, the suit, harness and helmet weighed about forty pounds and was speculated to have cost about $130,000.

These special protective pressurized suits were required because flying at 80,000 feet, hypoxia, or the decrease in the blood's oxygen, is a significant problem. The most common form of hypoxia, *hypoxic hypoxia*, is caused by a reduction of oxygen pressure in the lungs or exposure to high altitudes. As an example, the atmospheric pressure at 60,000 feet results in unconsciousness in eight to ten seconds and death within fifteen seconds. On a comparative basis, at the Blackbird's operational flight level of 80,000 feet, unconsciousness would ensue in approximately three to five seconds, and death in less than ten seconds.

Once suited and securely connected, the pilot and RSO were transferred to a portable oxygen unit for about thirty minutes prior to takeoff to filter out nitrogen and any external gas impact occurring during the suit up process reducing the possibility of decompression sickness. The O2 coolers in the transport van were hooked to the suits to keep the crew members cool until they were in the aircraft and connected to the air conditioning system. A pilot and RSO are transported in the PSD van, which looks plenty comfortable.

Getting the crew members into the air as soon as possible was the number one priority, but SSgt Fossett told me occasionally a plane equipment malfunction would occur and takeoff could be delayed from just few minutes up to three hours. This was a difficult and inconvenient situation because the crew members were fully pressurized and ready to fly. Waiting in the building or van in these bulky suits, hooked to the portable oxygen tanks and O2 cooling tubes for any length of time, tried a person's patience, and that was not an ideal mental attitude before flying a stressful mission. SSgt Fossett said that a long wait produced other problem such as the need to go to the bathroom. The UCD took care of a urination need, but if the need was to defecate, that became a problem. In that event, the PSD technicians had to go through the complete process of un-suiting and re-suiting again.

A pilot and RSO are transported in the PSD van.
(Courtesy US Air Force)

NASA research flight crew members in their pressure suits
look more like astronauts than a flight crew.
(Courtesy US Air Force)

27

IN THE COCKPIT

W hen flying other types of military aircraft, prior to takeoff the pilot inspected the plane to ensure there are no apparent problems, and after this final look, he or she climbs into the cockpit. However, the plane inspection process for the Blackbird pilot was quite different. Arriving at the hangar, or the "barn" as the crews referred to it, the pilot already in his fully pressurized flight suit was unable to made a visual check of the plane's exterior. The crew chief performed the "launch supervisory" inspection, identified and corrected any problem.

When the external launch supervisory pre-flight inspection was completed and the OK given by the crew chief, the pilot and RSO exited the transport van, shook hands with the ground crew, climbed the access ladder, shook hands with each other, and slid down into their ergonomic seats to settle in. Getting comfortable was extremely important because the space between the canopy rails didn't give much room to move around after they were strapped in.

Once the crew was in the cockpit, PSD technicians began connecting the pilot and RSO to the plane's life support equipment: the seat harness kit, radio communications, face heat and oxygen systems, parachute and egress system. In my interview, SSgt Fossett compared this process to connecting several sets of mixed color Lego° blocks together. "You have to know the blue set connects here, the green set connects there, and the red set interconnects the white set, and the orange set connects there. You can't lose track of anything at any time. Everything must be connected and positive proof tested."

Page 154 contains a copy from the declassified SR-71A Flight Manual,

Section II, Figure 2-1 detailing the procedure to follow when hooking up the pilot's and RSO's seat and pressure suits to safety and environmental control systems and the seat harness within the cockpit. After looking at this page of instructions, I understand SSgt Fossett's analogy of connecting several sets of Legos'®. When a PSD technician completed the suit hookups and verified proper function of each one, the techs changed places and conducted a double-check of all hookups. After the techs gave their approval, the pilot and RSO continued the cockpit pre-flight process.

I asked SSgt Fossett what happened if there was a mechanical problem making the connections. She laughed and replied, "You fixed it." She said a common problem was an 'O' ring failing to properly seal, requiring a new one, or possibly changing out the coupling. Because each mission was important, every effort was made to get the plane off the ground ASAP. Non-performance of a mission was not an option, and if the problem could not be corrected immediately, a back-up plane was used. SSgt Fossett said the decision to use a back-up plane required the concurrence of several supervisory levels, and on occasion, the Wing Commander.

Once the crew pre-flight check was complete and the pilot was ready to taxi, the PSD techs returned to the aircraft to perform their final task of removing the safety pins from the pilot's and RSO's main "D" ring seat ejection, and the safety cap for the explosive charge contained in the parachute. These items were retained until the plane returned and then re-installed. Regardless of the reason for flying, whether it was an operational mission, training purposes, or a demonstration, all must be in order.

Pilot and RSO customary handshake before the flight.
(Courtesy Brian Lockett Air-and-Space.com)

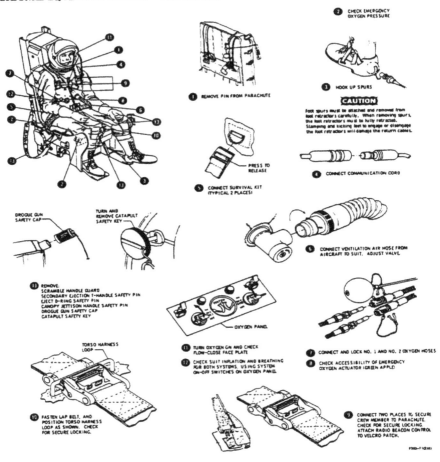

Pressure Suit Hookup Instructions from the Declassified SR-71A Flight Manual.
(Courtesy SR-71A On Line website, Paul R. Kucher)

28

WHEEL'S UP, THE SR-71A TAKE-OFF

Getting a Blackbird off the ground was no easy task. It required a coordinated effort on the part of the entire aviation operation groups involving; aircraft maintenance to ensure all mechanical components of the aircraft were in perfect working order, a crew chief and ground crew with an impeccable attention to detail, a logistics camera crew ensuring good working photo-grammetric survey/mapping camera equipment, mission planners, equipment tech reps, aircraft fuel system specialist, a weather forecasting team providing expected flight conditions, and airfield operations (control tower and air traffic control). Within these groups lived a special camaraderie and an unprecedented esprit de corps for the Blackbird program, unmatched by other flight groups. It only took two people to fly a Blackbird, but it took a hundred people to get it off the ground. The pilot states without hesitation that the success of a mission appears to belong to the flight crew when in reality it belongs to all the people who work within the program. The pilot and RSO just had the privilege to be the embodiment of all the work performed to make the mission a success.

Once in the cockpit and connected to support systems by PSD technicians, the pre-flight process of cockpit checks, ground, avionics and flight control checks, and camera readiness checks were completed. The crew chief, via the plane intercom, advises when all was ready to start the engines, at the pilot's discretion. As previously discussed, the Blackbird was powered by two Pratt & Whitney J58 jet engines, each capable of producing 32,500 pounds of thrust with afterburner giving it the capability of flying at speeds of more than sustained Mach 3+ (2,200 miles per hour, or more than three times the speed of sound). The YF-12 interceptor with a full 34,000 pounds of thrust, accelerated up to thirty-five miles per minute or 3,100 feet per second.

SR-71A side view with the Pratt & Whitney engine.
(Public Domain Photograph: Wolfkeeper)

THE ENGINE START UP PROCESS

The startup process was a coordinated effort between the pilot and ground crew. The first order of business for the ground crew was to chock the wheels. This was important because the SR-71A had no parking brake. It's hard to conceive that such a sophisticated plane with its high-technology equipment, had no parking brake.

After the required switches were activated in the proper sequence, "OK, start one," the pilot instructed the crew chief via the intercom, and subsequently "start two." According to technical information, the J-58 engine required a minimum of 680 horsepower just to start. An AG330 "start cart" powered by two Buick Wildcat V8 automobile engines, connected together using a single drive gearbox produced this required horsepower. The gearbox operated a vertical shaft which was inserted into an opening in the engine nacelle (the outer casing of the aircraft engine) to engage with the start pad. The Buick engine's gearbox would spin the vertical shaft, turning the turbines inside the engine. The photos on page 159 shows the retracted vertical shaft housed in the start cart, and the instrument control panel.

When the start cart turned the engines to about 3200 RPM, the pilot throttled from 'off' to 'idle' starting the fuel flowing, ready for the Triethylborane (TEB) to ignite the fuel. Ground crew members said when both start cart engines throttled up, it sounded like a drag race within an enclosed building. Then, when the two J-58 jet engines started, the noise level increased dramatically as it reverberated off the hangar walls. It was deafening!

Unfortunately, turning 3200 RPMs frequently overstressed these Buick engines, and research information indicates that, throwing a piston rod through the engine block was not an unusual event. The Buick engines were replaced around 1987 or 1988 by modified Chevrolet LS-7 454 engines which could better handle the stress. Eventually, these start carts were phased out in the Beale AFB hangars and replaced with permanent compressed air motor systems. However, the start carts continued to be used at remote operating locations.

Because of the extremely hot temperatures during flight, a special type Jet Propellant (JP-7) was developed. This fuel was different from regular jet fuel because it has a very high flash point of 60 degrees C (140 degrees F). Therefore, the JP-7 wouldn't catch fire even if you threw a lit match on it. The highly volatile TEB was used as a starter because it ignited spontaneously when it came in contact with air. By simultaneously injecting TEB into the turbine with the JP-7 fuel, it became, in reality, a controlled explosion to ignite the fuel. Now contemplate that for a moment. The plane was loaded with some 40,000 pounds of jet fuel, used two gasoline operated automobile engines and a small internal explosion to start the engines. Makes me nervous just to think about it, but pilot Lt. Col. Dave Fruehauf told me, "That was never a concern. There was no danger involved, it's just the way you started the engines. If everyone followed the established safety precautions and did their job properly, there was never a problem." TEB had a very distinct green flame which could be seen in the afterburners during engine start. The plane was loaded with some sixteen shots of TEB per engine to be used at incremental times during the flight; one at start up, one at takeoff, and one after each refueling when converting from normal power to afterburner. The pilot kept track of how many remaining shots of TEB were left via a small counter aft of each throttle.

AG 330 Start Cart contained two automobile engines.
(Photograph by Paul R. Kucher)

Two Buick or Chevrolet V8 engines were used in the Start Cart.
(Photograph by Paul R. Kucher)

The vertical shaft was inserted into an opening in the engine nacelle.
(Courtesy Mike Jetzer/heroicrelics.org)

The instrument panel controlling the synchronization of the two auto engines.
(Courtesy Mike Jetzer/heroicrelics.org)

Once both engines were started, the chocks were pulled from the wheels, the pilot advanced the throttle, gave a thumb up and a salute to say thanks to the ground crew, and the plane slowly starts to roll out of the hangar. Once the SR was cleared to taxi onto the runway, the mobile crew (the spare crew that did the preflight) drove down the runway looking for foreign object debris (FOD) that might be sucked into an engine or damage a tire. The special twenty-two ply B.F. Goodrich tires on the Blackbird were filled with nitrogen and inflated to 450 psi., making it imperative to avoid any potential puncture or blowout.

Remember, it has no parking brake, so on the runway the wheels were once again chocked. as the pilot completed the final engine run-up and trim and advised the control tower, ready to takeoff. After the mobile crew completed the runway sweep and the tower granted clearance, the chocks were pulled and the pilot throttled up. Once the afterburners kicked into full operation, the plane accelerated rapidly. In my research, some pilots indicated that because the afterburners in the Blackbird were asymmetrical, manual power had to be applied uniformly to both engines, otherwise it was difficult to maintain a straight center line takeoff. In my interviews with Lt. Col. Dave Fruehauf, he stated, "That was not a problem for a seasoned pilot. Although each plane responded a little differently, once you were accustomed to any peculiarities of the plane, center line control was pretty easy."

In an interview with USAF Staff Sergeant (SSgt) Preston Hillis, he told me, "At Kadena Air Base Okinawa, Japan, the Blackbird was always given takeoff priority. If our plane was not already cleared for takeoff, we waited, which we did frequently." SSgt. Hillis was a Loadmaster on a Military Air Transport Service (MATS) C-133 flying out of Dover AFB, Delaware. "We flew engines, equipment boxes, weapons, and supplies into Vietnam combat operations locations and remained on the ground just long enough to unload, pick up damaged equipment, and the silver cases containing the remains of fallen warriors, and headed back to Dover. Kadena AB was one of the first refueling points on our return flight, and our departure often coincided with the Blackbird schedule. We were anxious to take off and return home but watching the Blackbird was exciting and always worth the wait."

Thundering down the runway and feeling the energy generating from the two Pratt and Whitney turbojets with afterburners wide open gets the adrenaline pumping quickly. An experience that perhaps made the pilot feel more alive than anything else in life. Yes, anything!

At approximately 210 knots (240 mph), the SR-71 rotated and accelerated lifting off the runway shattering the relative quietness of the day. Anyone close by the runway knew when a Blackbird took off. The deafening sound of two J-58 engines with afterburners at full throttle was described as a freight train moving downhill while others say it was a bone rattling sound penetration. As a precaution, at Beale AFB, a T-38 chase plane was launched before the Blackbird takeoff, or was available to launch should there be any airborne problem. If necessary, the chase plane could easily fly over and under the Blackbird to view the exterior before the Blackbird continued on its mission.

As soon as the wheels were off the ground, the landing gear was retracted. In a matter of ten seconds the aircraft was in a thirty-five to forty-degree climb reaching an altitude of 25,000 feet in about three minutes. This rapid acceleration to acquire that altitude as quickly as possible was a precaution because in the event of an engine failure, the pilot would be able to maneuver the plane for a landing. The 'climbing to mission altitude' record was set by Lt. Col. Jim Sullivan who reached 80,000 feet at Mach 3 in just fourteen minutes. That, however, was the exception to normal takeoff procedure. As we will discuss in Chapter 29, the Blackbird required refueling shortly after takeoff and therefore had to level off to the altitude of the refueling tanker, which was about 25,000 feet. But that climb to 80,000 feet in fourteen minutes is certainly impressive.

A Blackbird flew on average once per week because of the turnaround time, and if maintenance or repairs rendered a plane unavailable to fly for any length of time, it became a concern. Because the Operating Location usually housed only three planes, the remaining two planes had to fly more frequently to compensate for the out-of-service plane, creating increased stress on the planes. Lt. Col. Dave Fruehauf said mission completion was priority one, and out of necessity he had flown the same plane twice in one week. Once airborne, the next important activity was to locate the KC-135 tanker and take on additional fuel.

SR-71B Number 831 takeoff showing full afterburner and shock diamonds.
(Courtesy NASA EC 92-1284)

29

HANGING ON THE BOOM

Unlike other jet aircraft, the Blackbird took off with only a partial fuel load to reduce weight and stress on the tires and ensure the plane could still successfully take off should one engine fail, and refueled within several minutes after takeoff. Because the Blackbird got extremely hot at high speeds and expanded in length about four inches with this heat buildup, the plane's panels were designed to fit loosely when cold. At a cruising speed of Mach 3, the increased heat made everything fit tighter but, on the ground, the plane dripped fuel everywhere. It was a nuisance, but ground crews became accustomed to that. In ground crew vernacular, if they were not careful, the plane would "pee" on them. It wasn't difficult to pick out the ground crew guys who had recently participated in a Blackbird takeoff. They smelled like JP-7 fuel, their hair looked slick and sticky, and their uniforms had fuel stains. Talk about "dirty jobs." In my research, I read that using a half can of Coke° in the wash removed all the stains and smells from the clothing. I wonder how someone discovered that?

A KC-135Q refueling tanker, with a capacity of some 31,000 gallons of fuel, took off thirty minutes or more ahead of the Blackbird to be in position for a rendezvous. These tankers were developed specifically to refuel the Blackbirds. Each tanker was equipped with a modified fuel tank system for retaining the JP-4 used by the KC-135Q itself and the special JP-7 supplied to the SR-71. This advance takeoff time was important not only for the tanker to be in place awaiting the arrival of the Blackbird with its limited amount of fuel, but also to check the weather conditions at the rendezvous point. The Blackbird was not equipped with weather radar, so it was totally dependent on the tanker's advice for satisfactory refueling conditions, or to change the refueling point.

The KC 135Q was equipped with a boom permitting Blackbird refueling at or near the tanker's maximum airspeed with minimum flutter. This refueling boom beneath the aft fuselage had the ability to transfer fuel at the rate of approximately 6,000 pounds per minute while cruising at 400 mph.

All air-to-air refueling was a time of great concentration for both the Blackbird pilot and the KC-135 boom operator. If the boom missed the intake receptacle it could result in damage to the plane, and a life-threatening situation for the crews of both planes. Therefore, the pilot and the boom operator were always on alert for anything that could go wrong.

The tanker crews were usually deployed to an operating location simultaneously with the Blackbirds they supported. The more often these crews worked together, the more harmonious their refueling methodology became. Over time, the tanker and the Blackbird crews formed a unique bond of trust, confidence and comradeship seldom found anywhere else. Unlike other tanker crews, these "Q crews" were exclusive to the SR-71, and the only crews with knowledge of the radio silent refueling procedures. Depending on location, at 25,000 feet and this speed, both the tanker and Blackbird were vulnerable during the refueling process. Therefore, absolute silence was often necessary. US Air Force retired Col. William L. Spacy flew KC-135-Qs out of Beale AFB for eight years. He posted this comment on the *Air Refueling Archive* website. "Early on, the Q tanker guys were looked down on. We were excused from Alert Duty, wouldn't tell anyone what we were doing, and got to go TDY [Temporary Duty] a lot! Until mid-1968 or so, we were the exclusive aerial refueling support for the A-12/SR-71A/YF-12 aircraft. The 903rd ARS had the only full Q tankers. It was my experience that the tanker fleet didn't always get the credit they earned. However, speak to some of the receivers about the value of the Gas Station at 26,000 feet, and usually they were happy to see us, especially 3,000 miles from the nearest runway."

The refueling intake receptacle on the Blackbird was located behind the RSO cockpit. The pilot maneuvered the Blackbird into the pre-contact position and opened the air-refueling door alerting the boom operator the Blackbird was ready to receive fuel. Maneuvering the Blackbird into position, the pilot carefully monitored the two rows of red and green lights on the underside of the KC-135 tanker to line up for a solid connection. The operator extended the boom and guided the nozzle into the receptacle. Once the nozzle was locked in the receptacle, the boom operator confirmed that contact was successful, the fuel was transferred. The SR-71A Flight Manual, Section II-figure 2-12 on page 168 provides a visual image of the connection process and indicates the variables for boom and receptacle contact. Comparing air-to-air refueling with other planes he had flown, Lt. Col. Fruehauf says, "The SR-71 was the easiest plane to refuel."

The KC-135Q was the first aircraft with a boom intercom permitting aircraft-to aircraft communication while maintaining radio frequency silence. Lt. Col. Fruehauf told me there was seldom any unnecessary intercom chatter between the Blackbird pilot and the tanker personnel. However, interjecting a bit of humor into the process and reflecting back on the days of full-service gas stations, I imagined a conversation where the boom operator said, "Welcome to the gas station. Hold steady and we will fill her up. Will that be regular or premium today?" The pilot responds, "Premium please, check the oil, and clean the bug splatters on the windshield while you are at it."

Hanging on the boom as the fuel flows, the pilot monitored the row of lights indicating the plane's vertical and horizontal position relative to the boom and maintained a speed of 348 knots (400 MPH) commensurate with the tanker. With six separate fuel tanks containing a full load of 80,280 pounds, the Blackbird was a flying gas tank between two engines. A copy of the SR-71A Flight Manual Section I, figure 1-32 on page 169 shows each tanks locations and capacity. It was literally a flying gas tank.

As the additional fuel increased the Blackbirds weight, it was necessary to increase the speed to keep up with the tanker. To compensate for the additional weight, the pilot left one engine at maximum military power and pushed the other engine into minimum afterburner. In about twelve to twenty minutes the Blackbird took on some 35,000 to 50,000 pounds of fuel. As a general rule, two tankers were needed to transfer the required amount of JP-7 fuel, and often a third tanker was available in case one of the tankers experienced an off-load problem. Before the refueling concluded, the Blackbird pilot communicated to the tanker pilot which direction he planned to turn after refueling. When completed, the boom automatically disconnected from the receptacle, and the boom operator began retraction. The refueling door was closed and the plane moved away from the tanker. Once clear, and the pilot received approval to climb to operating altitude, he throttled into afterburner mode and a shot of TEB was automatically dispensed to re-ignite the afterburners.

Not only did the Blackbird refuel shortly after takeoff, it required frequent refueling. Pumping fuel from three tanks simultaneously, the two engines used approximately 30,000 pounds of fuel per hour at cruise speed. As fuel was used, it was replaced with gas produced from liquid nitrogen tanks ensuring the atmosphere within the empty tank produced no negative reaction. Using fuel this fast, supersonic flying generally lasted no more than ninety minutes before the pilot had to refuel again. Putting that in perspective, however, this typically meant the Blackbird covered some 2,500 miles during that ninety-minute flying time. During the Blackbird's operational program, it is estimated that the KC-135s completed 25,862 aerial refueling operations.

A SR-71 refuels during the linear aerospike experiment.
(Courtesy NASA EC 97-44295-114)

A KC-135 Stratotanker extends the refueling boom waiting on a SR-71.

Positioning the SR-71 to make a refueling connection.
(Courtesy US Air Force)

KC-135 AIR REFUELING BOOM LIMITS

NOTE
Tanker automatic disconnect
occurs at boundary of
gray areas.

CAUTION

Tanker auto-disconnect
limits do not apply when
receiver using manual
boom latching

Also see T.O. 1-1C-1

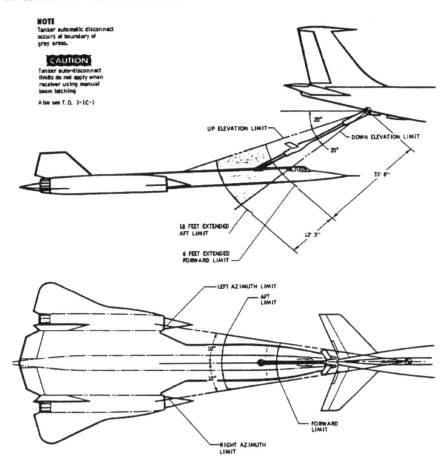

Boom limitations from the declassified SR-71A Flight Manual.
(Courtesy SR-71A On Line website, Paul R. Kucher)

FUEL QUANTITY

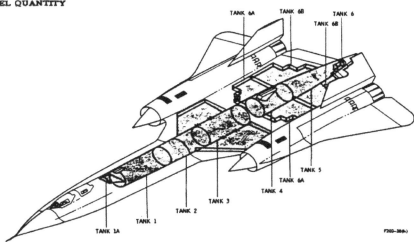

FUEL TANK CAPACITIES
Normal Flight Attitude

Tank	Fuel/Gal	Fuel (JP-7)
1A	251.1	1650 lb.
1	2095.9	13770 lb.
2	1974.1	12970 lb.
3	2459.7	16160 lb.
4	1453.6	9550 lb.
5	1758.0	11550 lb.
6A (forward)	1158.3	7610 lb.
6B (Aft)	1068.5	7020 lb.
Total	12219.2	80280 lb. *

* At average fuel density of 6.57 lb./gal.
(46.2° API, Fuel temperature = 78° F)

The SR-71 fuel tank locations and quantities from SR-71A declassified Flight Manual.
(Courtesy SR-71A On Line website, Paul R. Kucher)

30

IN-FLIGHT DINING. WHAT'S FOR DINNER?

For many people, eating a meal before or while flying is not recommended. The impact on our internal system as a result of takeoff, cabin pressure changes or air turbulence may cause us to feel nauseated, sending us reaching for an airsickness bag. Conversely, once in the air and with the airplane stabilized, it is nice to have a cold drink and perhaps a snack during the flight. Many commercial aircraft passengers remember the time when a full meal was served to both first class and coach passengers on most every domestic flight. However, the pilot and RSO were in a pressurized suit and unable to lift their visor to eat or drink, so, what did they do should they get hungry or thirsty during their mission? Well, I discovered they had both food and drink available.

Originally, special prepared liquidized food in sealed aluminum containers, similar to a toothpaste tube, was produced by the baby food manufacturer Gerber®. The Blackbird pilot and RSO were offered their choice of several tube food options such as; chicken-a-la-king, mac-n-cheese, chicken tortilla soup, beef and gravy, butterscotch or chocolate pudding, applesauce, or peaches. Sounds like any of those would give me indigestion at 80,000 feet and Mach 3, but apparently Gerber perfected a formula not only to accommodate a baby's sensitive digestive system, but also for these high-flying crew members. So, what is the favorite food for today's U-2 pilots? Chicken-a-la-king and caffeinated chocolate pudding tops the list. The cost of each tube of food has been estimated at twenty-five dollars.

An article posted on the US Army website states that tube food for the U-2 program is produced only by the Department of Defense Combat

Feeding Directorate (CFD) at Natick Soldier Research, Development and Engineering Center. The CFD supplies U-2 pilots with approximately 28,000 tubes annually, and has done so for the past five decades. According to the CFD chef and physical science technician, no other company does what CFD is doing.

To access the food, a long feeding tube was screwed onto the food container tube, puncturing the seal. The feeding tube was then inserted into a special port on the right side of the helmet, as shown on the photo on page 172, and with a few gentle squeezes, the liquid food began to flow. Yum! Yum! Although several food tubes were available during the mission, crew members limited their food intake to a minimum because unless an emergency situation developed during the flight, defecating in the body suit was prohibited. A launch and recovery technician at the 9th Physiological Support Squadron, Beale AFB said U-2 pilots on average, consume one tube an hour.

As previously stated, the cockpit temperature was not a controlled environment. Thus, the contents of the food container tube were cold and often difficult to swallow; so, Pilot Colonel Rich Graham discovered an "in-flight oven" to heat up the tube. "If I took that tube and held it against the window in the front windscreen which was probably between 300 and 350 F for about a minute and half on each side, it warmed up the tube and the contents. It went down a lot better warm than it did cold." It wasn't like home, but you improvised and made do until you could get back home. What's that old saying that necessity is the mother of invention? Well, once again that proved to be true.

Water, a caffeine supplement, and a sports drink mix, were also available to help keep the crew hydrated. The amount of liquid intake was not as much a concern as food because of the UCD discussed in Chapter 26.

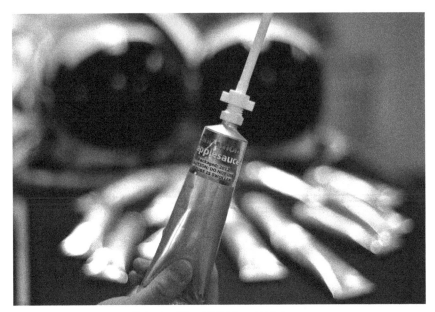

Tube food For SR-71A and U-2 Crew.
(Courtesy US Air Force-Beale AFB)

Food tube inserted in helmet port.
(Courtesy US Air force-Beale AFB)

31

WHAT A VIEW!

The progression to attain higher altitudes was an achievement within itself; however, taking a photograph at an altitude of 80,000 feet yielding details of objects as small as 2.5 feet is difficult to conceive. In Chapter 10, we noted the U-2 photographic demonstration at President Eisenhower's farm from 60,000 feet showing not only his cattle, but also their feeding troughs. The only basis of comparison for most of us is flying in a commercial airliner at 25,000 to 30,000 feet. At that altitude we can make out land divisions, but it is difficult to discern many details. The highest altitude recorded for a commercial flight was set by the British-French Concorde, which ascended to 60,000 feet but visibility from within the plane was very restricted, as it is in most airplanes.

With the need for high altitude flying, the US Air Research and Development Command mandated modifications to the RB-57D Canberra reconnaissance plane, increasing the operating ceiling from 48,000 to 64,000 feet. This provided additional reconnaissance capabilities but unfortunately not from vulnerability. The Soviet Union's improved radar technology could track aircraft flying above 65,000 feet, and soon their SAMs would be capable of reaching that altitude. The Lockheed CL-282 U-2 increased the altitude to 70,000 feet followed by the A-12 Oxcart operating at up to 85,000 feet, and the SR-71 which could reach an altitude of 90,000 feet.

The minimum altitude to see the beginning of the earth's curvature is 35,000 to 37,000 feet (seven miles) therefore, any curvature visibility will be very slight even at 37,000 feet. Blackbird crew members say that looking out the canopy at 80,000 feet is a magnificent sight. The curvature of the Earth could be seen about three hundred fifty miles in all directions. At this altitude, the sky is deep indigo blue because 97% of the atmosphere which gives the sky its beautiful blue color, is well below the plane. This color contrast is indicated in the following photos.

A SR-71A at its working altitude.
(Courtesy US Air Force)

A SR-71A view of the earth from 83,000 feet.
(Courtesy Brian Shul, US Air Force)

32

LANDING THE BLACKBIRD

A pilot's landing philosophy is; any landing you can walk away from is a good landing and any landing you can walk away from and the plane can fly again is a great landing. As with any aircraft, landing the Blackbird was a critical event. In an interview with former Blackbird pilot Lt. Col. Dave Fruehauf, he related an unsettling landing experience during his third training flight. On Thursday 11 January 1968 during a local training flight out of Beale AFB, he and Instructor Pilot, Lt. Col. Robert G. Sowers, experienced a double generator failure in SR-71B, 61-7957. Without electrical power from the generators, cavitation occurred, disrupting the fuel flow to the engines resulting in a double engine flame out. Having lost the ability to control the aircraft, they ejected at 3,000 feet only seven miles from the end of the runway at Beale. Both the pilots survived the bailout, but there was nothing left of the Blackbird. Lt. Col. Fruehauf said it was a memory never to be forgotten.

Because the Blackbird had no flaps to produce drag, controlling the airspeed and ensuring that the rate of descent was stabilized was critical. To systematically reduce altitude and speed, a standard landing pattern was developed, and a copy of these instructions from the SR-71A Flight Manual, Section II, Figure 2-16, is included on page 179. The aircraft was aligned with the runway center line as the final approach began. The landing gear in the down position with green lights illuminated on the instrument panel indicated all wheels were deployed and in a locked position. Watching the runway approach lights in the distance, the objective was to be 175 knots (201 mph) over the fence, closing on the runway.

As soon as the wheels touched the runway the pilot throttled back and deployed a large orange drag chute to reduce speed. Utilization of the drag chute reduced the distance to final stop to about 5,000 feet. If the chute failed to properly deploy, the stopping distance increased to about 10,000 feet. Unless there were crosswind concerns or braking system problems, when the plane decelerated to fifty-five knots (sixty-three mph) the pilot jettisoned the chute to preclude any aircraft damage. The maintenance truck following the aircraft retrieved the chute and transported it back to the parachute shop for inspection, repacking and future use.

What happens without the drag chute, you ask? Well, consider this experience. According to research information, on 20 July 1972 SR-71A, tail number 64-17978, nicknamed "Rapid Rabbit," attempting a landing at Kadena AB ahead of an off-shore typhoon with crosswinds of thirty-five knots. The pilot, Capt. Dennis K. Bush, deployed the drag chute, but unfortunately it collapsed. Realizing one of the tires had exploded on impact, Capt. Bush jettisoned the chute, re-ignited the afterburners and quickly climbed back into the air. On the subsequent touchdown, the left-side tires caught fire, and the right-side tires blew out. The Blackbird slid down the runway until the landing gears collapsed. When the wing struck the runway, the left engine exploded causing the plane to gyrate down the runway totally destroying the fuselage. The fire and safety crews were on the spot immediately and fortunately the pilot and the RSO, Capt. James W. Fagg escaped without injury. Another unforgettable event.

When safely on the ground, the Blackbird followed a mobile unit and taxied back to the hangar. When the plane came to a full stop; the wheels were chocked, and via the intercom, the crew chief gave the OK for engine shut down. With the throttles stop-cocked, switches, radio and electronic equipment were turned off. The canopy yawned open and the waiting PDS techs disconnected the safety harness and life support systems connections and the pilot and RSO egress the plane onto the boarding platform.

Although the plane's exterior cooled during the deceleration, the landing gear and engine exhaust system often remained heated, taking a while longer for a complete cool down. Brian Lockett, owner of *The Air and Space Museum* internet site, made the observation that in 1964, after performing several flybys at Edwards Air Force Base, a Blackbird taxied back into the hangar with the engine exhaust system still warm enough that a small breeze over it set off the fire sprinkler system.

As soon as the plane was secure, the ground crew retrieved the on-board

Mission Recording System (MRS) tape and the camera's film and provided them to the Strategic Information Office for processing and photographic interpretation. The PSD techs involved in the plane's launch were there for the return of the plane. After the flight crew exited the aircraft, the techs assisted them into the waiting transport van and connected their suits to the O2 coolers. The techs returned to the plane, reinstalled the safety pins from the pilot and RSOs main "D" ring seat ejection, and the safety cap for the explosive charge contained in the parachute. They collected the water containers and food tubes from the cockpit. On the flight information sheet, the techs recorded any reported, or apparent, issues or problems with the flight suits for future analysis and evaluation.

The pilot and RSO were transported to the PSD facility to un-suit, shower and change into their orange flight suits. Once again PSD technicians assisted in the suit's removal. The suit, helmet, and gloves were taken to the pre-flight room where a preliminary inspection was made and if no problems were discovered, returned to the storage unit awaiting the detailed inspection, and cleaning prior to the next flight of this crew.

During an interview with former Blackbird pilot Lt. Col. Ed Yeilding, he said it was not unusual for a VIP tour group to be present to observe the suit-up and/or the un-suiting procedure. On one occasion at Beale AFB, a tour group was present when he and the RSO returned to the PSD building to un-suit after a mission. Ed says the RSO had experienced a small diarrhea problem during the mission but didn't think much about it. They took off their pressure suits, stood up in their full body white underwear, smiled, waived to the group and turned to go into the locker room to shower. Unbeknownst to the RSO, the seat of his underwear was brown from the diarrhea problem. Ed said, "I can imagine what these observers thought. Man, that must have been some scary mission!"

After a shower and getting re-dressed, the pilot and RSO, with mission notes in hand, were off to flight operations and maintenance debriefings while the flight information was still fresh in their minds. This was the time to discuss the entire mission from liftoff to landing; the good, the bad and anything ugly. This "lessons learned" debriefing process was an integral part to the success of the next mission.

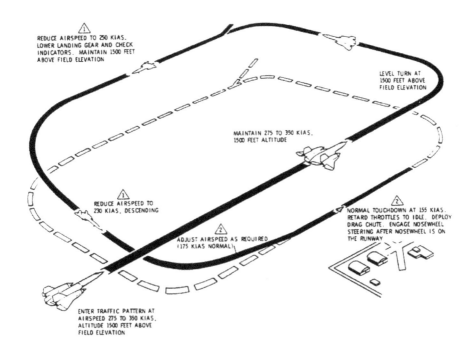

REDUCE AIRSPEED TO 250 KIAS.
LOWER LANDING GEAR AND CHECK
INDICATORS. MAINTAIN 1500 FEET
ABOVE FIELD ELEVATION

LEVEL TURN AT
1500 FEET ABOVE
FIELD ELEVATION

MAINTAIN 275 TO 350 KIAS,
1500 FEET ALTITUDE

REDUCE AIRSPEED TO
230 KIAS, DESCENDING

NORMAL TOUCHDOWN AT 155 KIAS.
RETARD THROTTLES TO IDLE. DEPLOY
DRAG CHUTE. ENGAGE NOSEWHEEL
STEERING AFTER NOSEWHEEL IS ON
THE RUNWAY

ADJUST AIRSPEED AS REQUIRED
(175 KIAS NORMAL)

ENTER TRAFFIC PATTERN AT
AIRSPEED 275 TO 350 KIAS,
ALTITUDE 1500 FEET ABOVE
FIELD ELEVATION

NOTE

1. For aircraft over 100,000 lbs. (more than 40,000 lb. fuel remaining),
maintain 275 KIAS on downwind leg and 250 KIAS on base leg; and use
an angle of attack of approximately 10.5° for final approach and landing.

2. Increase normal speed for final approach (175 KIAS) and landing
(155 KIAS) by 1 knot per 1000 lb of fuel over 10,000 lb remaining.
For maximum performance, the minimum landing speed is 10 KIAS less
than the speed determined by this rule. See Appendix figure A2-15.
The minimum final approach speed is 20 KIAS above the intended landing speed.

Standard landing pattern from the declassified SR-71A Flight Manual
Typical landing pattern.
(Courtesy SR-71A On Line website, Paul R. Kucher)

33

BLACKBIRD 64-17972
SETS THE WORLD SPEED RECORD

As the SR-71 program drew to a close, one by one the planes were decommissioned and stored, or moved to a new home, and so it was for Blackbird tail number 64-17972. On 6 March 1990 this test plane made the final trip from its 1966 birthplace at plant number forty-two in Palmdale, California to Washington-Dulles International Airport. It was decommissioned and retired from active service, officially bringing the era to an end and making the very last US military flight of the Blackbird.

The next duty station for 64-17972 was the Smithsonian National Air and Space Museum's Steven F. Udvar-Hazy Center in Chantilly, Virginia, where it occupies a place of prominence and will be admired for years to come. This Blackbird had served the US well in its mission to reform reconnaissance and became a beautiful, mysterious symbol of strength for the preservation of freedom. It deserved honor and respect for the important flights it made and the intrinsic value of the strategic information it provided from the reconnaissance missions it flew.

Blackbird number 64-17972's assembly started 13 December 1965, and the aircraft was rolled out on 15 September 1966. Its first flight was 12 December 1966 and over the course of twenty-four years, it flew 2801.1 hours. It became the official Lockheed Martin test plane on 24 January 1985, replacing SR-71 number 61-7955, a test plane which never flew an operational mission. After its service was completed, 61-7955 was placed on display at the Air Force Flight Test Center Museum at Edwards AFB, Califoirnia. Its final location was synonymous with its service purpose.

Lt. Col. "Ed" Yeilding, pilot, and Lt. Col. "JT" Vida, RSO, were selected to make this historical flight to the Smithsonian. Both men were seasoned airmen assigned to the Palmdale Plant 42 Flight Test Facility.

While in the SR-71 program, Lt. Col. Yeilding had 785 flying hours and ninety-three overseas reconnaissance missions to his credit. Lt. Col. Vida with 1,392.7 flying hours, accumulated more flying time than any pilot or RSO in the history of the Blackbird. Not only were they asked to deliver 64-17972 to the Smithsonian, but to set an aircraft speed record if possible, to call attention to the retirement of the Blackbird.

The Washington-Dulles flight plan was to fly almost due west over the Pacific, climb to 27,000 feet and circle back East to rendezvous with KC-135Q refueling tankers. With a solid refueling connection, they began to take on fuel. After experiencing a problem with one tank's fuel gauge, a determination was made that sufficient fuel was available for the flight, irrespective of what the gauge indicated. After refueling was completed and disengaged from the tanker, Lt. Col. Yeilding pushed the throttles forward, a shot of TEB dispensed to ignite the afterburners and this epic flight began.

At 0600 they passed over the west gate, a radar reference point over Oxnard on the southern California coast, the timer started. Away they flew, but a bit faster than the "down of a thistle" of Santa's sleigh. Mach 2.3 and 65,000 feet was soon reached as the Blackbird continued to climb, increasing speed as it streaked across the sky.

In an *Areoteck News* interview several years ago, recalling that early morning flight, Lt. Col. Yeilding said, "It was just breaking daylight on the West coast when we started our flight but enough light to see the white capped waves along the California coastline. Below the plane I could see the lights of Los Angeles. To the north I could see the San Francisco city lights and to the south, the lights at San Diego. What a spectacular sight, three cities in one view"

The Blackbird streaked across the sky 76,000 feet at Mach 3.3 in a slow cruse climb for fuel efficiency, literally flying faster than a rifle bullet. When a Blackbird reached or exceeded subsonic speed, people could hear its sonic boom breaking the sound barrier, and a few were lucky enough to see the plane, if only for a few seconds. In an interview with USAF Senior Master Sergeant (SMSgt) Albert "Al" Virden, a communications specialist in the 6903rd Security Squadron stationed at Osan AB Korea in 1970, he told me this story about his one-time, almost sighting of a Blackbird.

He and a few of his peers learned confidentially that the Blackbird would fly over Osan on a certain day. When the radar system operators spotted the plane on radar, they relayed to SMSgt Virden that the fly-over would occur in a couple of minutes. In an air of urgency, SMSgt Virden and friends rushed outside, excited to have the unique opportunity to see the Blackbird. After great anticipation, and to their dismay, they did not see the plane, not even a speck in the sky, just what appeared to be a very faint con-trail where it had passed, and that may have been an illusion. SMSgt Virden said jokingly, they agreed it took three people to view a flying Blackbird, "One to tell you it was in-bound, one to tell you it is here and one to tell you it was gone." I guess singing the 1926 song by American composer Ray Henderson and lyricist Mort Dixon, "Pack up all my care and woe, here I go, singing low. Bye, Bye blackbird" would have been appropriate for Al and his friends as they returned to their work stations.

At the top of their cruise altitude of 83,000 feet, the afterburners were terminated, the Blackbird crossed the east coast at supersonic speed, and started a descending left turn back into Washington DC. The directive given to Lt. Col. Yeilding was to make only one low approach at Dulles, and he wanted to make it memorable for the observers. He made a flyby at just under 200 feet, lighting the afterburners to let the crowd hear and feel the power of those J58 engines, and see the beauty of those bright orange flames behind that beautiful black airplane. As specified in the copy of the SR-71A Flight Manual landing instructions on page 179, a hard deck of 1500 feet above field elevation was a normal approach pattern. So, the 200 feet at which the Blackbird was flying really made some noise. The crowd was thrilled as it watched the Blackbird once again climb into the sky, displaying the afterburner shock diamonds.

The landing was smooth and Lt. Col. Yeilding parked the aircraft at the appropriate location. On the ground a crowd of people including USAF personnel, VIPs and other dignitaries gathered to welcome 64-17972 to its final destination. Lt. Col. Yeilding said as he and Lt. Col. Vida deplaned and shook hands, "We felt a mixture of emotions, excited that we had just flown the world's fastest airplane and set some new speed records yet feeling very sad because that would be our last flight in the marvelous Blackbird and the last time that beautiful Blackbird would ever fly."

The trip from Palmdale AFB, California to Washington-Dulles, 2,404 statute miles, took just a bit over one hour, setting a coast-to-coast record. A quick calculation revealed an average speed of 2,125 miles per hour. The MRS authenticated that speed and a time of sixty-seven minutes and fifty-four seconds for the record book. *The Air & Space Magazine* reported that at one point during the flight, the Air Force clocked the

SR-71 at 2,242.48 miles per hour. In total, four speed records were set on this flight. The United States National Aeronautic Association, the agency that verifies official aviation records, recorded these speed records, decimals rounded, on this historic flight.

1. Coast-to-Coast: 67 minutes 54 seconds, 2404 miles, average speed 2125 mph.
2. Los Angeles to Washington DC: 64 minutes 20 seconds, 2300 miles, average speed 2145 mph.
3. Kansas City to Washington DC: 26 minutes seconds, 942 miles, average speed 2176 mph.
4. St Louis to Cincinnati: 8 minutes 32 seconds, 311 miles, average speed 2190 mph.

Considering this new coast-to-coast record of sixty-seven minutes, it is interesting to look back to see the progression of aviation speed technology. On 16 July 1957, Marine Corps Major John Glenn took off from Los Alamitos Naval Air Station in California in his F8U Crusader. Three hours, twenty-three minutes, eight seconds, and three air refuelings later, he landed at Floyd Bennett Field in Brooklyn, New York, setting a transcontinental speed record of 725 mph. Major Glenn named the flight "Project Bullet" because the Crusader flew faster than a shot fired from a .45-caliber pistol. What a difference thirty-three years make.

However, this was not the first speed record set by 64-17972. On 1 September 1974, this plane set a world speed record flying from New York to London, England, a distance of 3,461 statute miles, in one hour, fifty-four minutes, and fifty-six seconds. The average speed was 1807 mph, slowing only once for refueling. At the controls for this speed record was pilot Major James V. Sullivan and RSO Major Noel F. Widdifield

On 13 September 1974, this plane set a world record, flying 5446 statute miles from London to Los Angeles in three hours, forty-seven minutes and thirty-nine seconds with an average speed of 1435 mph. Capt. Harold B. "Buck" Adams was the pilot and Maj. William C. Machorek the RSO. Another first for this aircraft was that of being displayed at the Farnborough United Kingdom Air Show. It was the first time a Blackbird had been on public display outside of the United States.

Setting this speed record to the Smithsonian National Air and Space Museum was the perfect finish for this legendary aircraft.

The Final Landing for Blackbird 64-17972.
Pilot, Lt. Col. "Ed" Yeilding and RSO, Lt. Col. "JT" Vida.
(Courtesy US Air Force)

34

THE END OF THE BEGINNING

The Last Blackbird to fly, NASA number 844, with chase plane.
(Courtesy NASA EC 99-45065-1)

During WWII, the Allies were victorious at El Alamein (23 October – 11 November 1942) driving General Rommel's German troops out of Egypt, marking a turning point in the war. In a speech celebrating the victory at London's Mansion House November 1942, Prime Minister Winston Churchill made this observation, "The Germans have received back again that measure of fire and steel which they have so often meted out to others. Now this is not the end. It is not even the beginning of the end. But it is, perhaps, the end of the beginning."

The end of the Cold War in 1991 eventually brought to an end the aggressive Cold War spy plane activity. For practical purposes, the U-2 program was sidelined when the A-12 was activated in 1963. The A-12 program ended in 1968 with the activation of the SR-71 Blackbird, and SR-71-NASA number 844 made the final flight on Saturday, 9 October 1999 at the Edwards AFB air show ending the SR-71 program. As evidenced over many decades, these Cold War reconnaissance planes were just the end of the beginning of overhead espionage.

Despite the valuable intelligence gathered by the Blackbird, its "operating cost" was substantially more than any other aircraft. Some estimate the cost of operating just the plane up to $50,000 per flying hour, increasing to $100,000 per hour when the incremental support was included. That's about $500,000 for a five-hour mission. The comparable cost to operate the U-2 was estimated at $30,813 per flying hour. As you would expect, "maintenance cost" for the Blackbird was also very high. The feature article in April 2018 issue of *Combat Aircraft* estimated that approximately 735 maintenance man-hours per flight were required in 1968. However, through experience and increased system reliability, that number was reduced to 125 by the end of the program. Some government agencies were uncomfortable spending this much money on gathering intelligence when other available reconnaissance methods were more economical. In the spring of 1988, US Air Force Secretary Edward C. Aldridge revealed the SR-71 fleet total operating and maintenance cost was comparable to the cost of maintaining two tactical fighter wings. Not surprisingly, plans to retire the SR-71 program were announced in 1989.

When the U-2, and subsequently the Blackbird, were introduced, high altitude flying was the only way to secure accurate reconnaissance information. With the introduction of satellite reconnaissance capability, the question of whether or not to continue to operate the expensive SR-71 became the primary consideration for both military leaders and politicians. US satellites were far superior in operational reliability and required less funding, however they were very predictable. Their flight patterns were easy to determine, creating the opportunity for an enemy to hide equipment, inventory and activity much easier than when the Blackbirds were flying.

The decision was made in mid-1990 to close the 9th Recon Squadron. However, since spy planes still provided a tactical advantage in gathering intelligence on other nations, a few Blackbirds were retained for limited use despite the maintenance and budgetary issues, and the remaining aircraft were sent to static display locations. Appalled by the decision to scuttle the Blackbird program, Senator John Glenn (D-Ohio) an avid proponent of the program, denounced its termination in his 7 March 1990 speech on the Senate floor which included these remarks, ".... In retiring the SR-71, the United States has essentially removed itself from the strategic aerial reconnaissance business. Intelligence systems such as the SR-71 are the eyes and ears for our nation's defense and are therefore true force-multipliers.... Termination of the SR-71 was a grave mistake and could place our nation at a serious disadvantage in the event of a future crisis...."

The design plans for the Blackbird were sought after so diligently by foreign governments that the government ordered Lockheed to destroy them and the tooling required to produce the plane. The Blackbird program was briefly revived in 1997 and a small number of training flights were made, but funding was zeroed out and the program officially ended in 1998.

The last Blackbird flight was made on Saturday, 9 October 1999 at the Edwards AFB air show. The aircraft used was SR-71 61-7980, NASA number 844. NASA Research Pilot Rogers E. Smith and Flight Test Engineer Robert R. Meyer, Jr. were at the controls. The Blackbird flew Mach 3.21 at 80,100 feet on its final run. It was scheduled to make another flight the following day, but a fuel leak grounded the aircraft, preventing it from flying again. This final flight ended the era of the high-altitude reconnaissance SR-71 spy plane. NASA Blackbird number 844 is on display inside the main gate at NASA Dryden Flight Research Center at Edwards AFB, California.

Because the U-2 was far more economical to operate than the SR-71 and more quickly adaptable to reconnaissance requirements, today it continues to fly missions over Iraq, Syria, Afghanistan, and other locations. The USAF reports that since 1994, $1.7 billion dollars has been spent to modernized the U-2 airframe with new sensors and cameras. These modifications also involved the conversion to the GE F-118 engine, and a re-designation from the U-2 to the U-2S. Additionally, the U-2s gained the ability to transmit photographic images back to land-based centers in real time, making them an important asset in fighting terrorism. The 9th Reconnaissance Wing, Beale Air Force Base, California, continues to be the home base for the U-2s, with worldwide deployment to operational detachments on a rotation basis. As of 2105, the USAF reported thirty-three active U-2s.

The genius of Kelly Johnson and his team of slide-rule engineers taught the avionics world many impressive lessons well before the advent of computer technology. They developed new concepts, invented fabrication methods and designed tools to create the incredible SR-71 Blackbird. This plane played a vital part in keeping America safe during a very difficult time, and Lockheed employees were proud to have been a small part of that process. Although the Blackbird has not been an active contributor to our reconnaissance program for a long time, its legacy will live on for many years. In all reality, it is the essence of a legend.

The SR-71A Blackbird Statistical Data
Published by the Dryden Flight Research Center

Manufacturer: Lockheed Aircraft Corp.
Length: 107.4 feet
Height: 18.5 feet
Wingspan: 55.6 feet
Air Frame Material: Titanium
Gross Takeoff Weight: 140,000 pounds, including fuel weight of 80,000 pounds
Maximum Weight: 170,000 pounds
Power Plants: Two Pratt and Whitney J58 axial-flow turbojets with afterburners, each producing up to 32,500 pounds of thrust with afterburners (equal to the engines in an ocean liner)
Fuel Consumption: Engines burned 44,000 pounds of fuel per hour, refueling every 90 minutes
Range: 2500 to 3200 nautical miles before refueling
Cruise Speed: Mach 3.2 (over three times the speed of sound)
Maximum Speed: Mach 3.5, (the official record, set in July of 1976 was 2,193.13 mph)
Maximum Altitude: 90,000 feet but typically operated at 70,000 feet
Paint: Over 60 pounds of high-heat emission black paint were used to cover each plane
Windows: The cockpit windows were covered in quartz for protection during high altitude and speed
Cost: $33 million per plane in the 1960s
Missions: A total of 3,551 mission sorties for a total of 17,294 hours were flown during the Cold War

Number of Blackbirds shot down: None. It is estimated that more than four thousand missiles were fired at them while flying these missions.

Number of Blackbirds damaged by enemy fire: None

Hours of operation: According to historical records, the fleet of Blackbirds logged a combined total of 53,490 hours of flight time, of which 11,675 had been flown at Mach 3 or above.

Last SR-71A Flight: Saturday 9 October 1999, at the Edwards AFB air show. The aircraft used was NASA 844, number 61-7980

35

THE FUTURE OF OVERHEAD ESPIONAGE

The ending of these Cold War spy plane programs in no way indicated that overhead espionage was no longer needed. Just the opposite was true. As referenced in Chapter 34, it is just the end of the beginning. Reconnaissance has become such an integral part of ongoing US national security, the need for it will continue into the foreseeable future. Today, it appears that any nation, notwithstanding how impoverished it may be, that desires to have nuclear weapons can acquire them. For example, in 1998 Pakistan's per capita income was only $470 when it acquired nuclear capability. According to Bloomberg Economics, North Korea's 2017 annual per capita income was approximately $1,800, about half the amount in Vietnam, and yet North Korea spends massive amounts to pursue greater nuclear capability. This type determination to possess nuclear weapons in an unstable world environment creates the necessity to continually monitor their nuclear capabilities and whether or not they are ready for use. Advanced spy technology capabilities changed the way we view the world, and the world's view of us.

In the 1950s and 60s, the United States was the global leader in the amount of money allocated for research and development accounting for approximately two thirds of the total amount spent by all nations. That was not the case in 2017. China expanded its spy technology and weapons research development substantially, and now runs a close second to the US in spending. Despite their unstable economy, Russia, North Korea and Iran also increased their research spending, and the expectation is that will be continued into the future. Russia, even with its weak economic condition, continues to be a world nuclear power leader. Russian President Vladimir

Putin, speaking to a group of Russian military leaders noted that during the Cold War, Russia lagged behind the US in the development and use of the atomic bomb and ICBMs, but after making military modernization its top priority. Russia now leads the world in developing a new class of weapons.

The US also has far more reconnaissance competition in the twenty-first century. During the past two decades overhead reconnaissance has become accepted among several nations. It occurs with some regularity through satellites, making it necessary to be cognizant of any activity which could be surveilled at any time. Although many countries previously did not have a dedicated spy plane, in recent years Russia, Israel, India, the United Kingdom, Germany, and France have developed and deployed satellites used for both intelligence gathering and communication relay purposes. We have entered an age in which we cannot afford to look away, or even blink, for fear our adversaries will gain an advantage over our capabilities. Game-changing technology uses of space satellites, information technology, advanced imaging capabilities, drones, and other electronic surveillance options now provide a large percentage of our reconnaissance needs, However, while satellites are much less expensive to operate, they have limitations such as; predictability, time needed to get to a target, and inability to take a second quick look. They do not operate on a demand basis, but a pre-set orbital program and while they are effective in many ways, one could make an argument that a high-altitude plane is needed in addition to the satellites. Because the U-2 was so much more efficient to operate than the SR-71, in 2015 the Air Force re-activated it and continues to operate it today for reconnaissance purposes to augment the reconnaissance satellites.

As during the Cold War, the US incurs a significant risk if it does not continue to develop and utilize all options available to remain militarily superior to its adversaries. That said, in March 2018, Russia announced the operational readiness of a nuclear-capable, air-launched, hypersonic Intercontinental Ballistic Missile (ICBM) named the Kinzhal. According to Russia, it can carry either a nuclear or conventional warhead, fly ten times the speed of sound, and has a range of more than 1,250 miles. Russia also noted that another new ICBM, the Avangard, would be ready for use in December, 2019. Russia says this ICBM flies at twenty times the speed of sound and with its ability to change course or altitude while in flight, it can defy existing missile defense systems. Over the past few years, the US has been working to develop hypersonic weapons, but it appears that any implementation is still several years away. Meanwhile, the US continues its overhead espionage work to monitor, confirm and validate the Russian data.

USAF X-37B space plane landing at NASA's Kennedy Space Center.
(Courtesy US Air Force)

Research sources indicate that the US Air Force has successfully launched and retrieved a reusable unmanned space plane known as the Boeing X-37 Orbital Test Vehicle. This space plane with its wingspan of some fifteen feet is propelled into space via a rocket, but glides back to earth like the space shuttle. NASA began the X-37 development project in 1999 and subsequently turned it over to the DOD in 2004. The space plane's first orbital mission launched on 22 April 2010 and its fourth mission launched 20 May 2015. It landed at Kennedy Space Flight Center on 8 May 2017 after 718 days in space. Amateur astronomers have detected and tracked the orbital flight pattern of the X-37, which appears to include flying over North Korea, Iraq, Iran, Pakistan and Afghanistan, creating the suspicion that it is possibly being used for surveillance, although that has not been confirmed.

US Air Force RQ-4A Global Hawk.
(Courtesy US Air Force)

A major part of today's overhead espionage, is the Northrop Grumman US Air Force RQ-4A Global Hawk drone at a cost of some $120 million each. This drone provides real-time intelligence, surveillance and reconnaissance missions. The Global Hawk is a high-altitude, unmanned, aircraft which provides day and night real time surveillance and reconnaissance through imagery and signals intelligence, and moving target indicator sensors. Although its speed is only 357 mph, it can cover 12,300 nautical miles with an endurance time of more than thirty-four hours. The "R" is for reconnaissance and the "Q" denotes it is unmanned. This sophisticated drone has demonstrated its usefulness during several reconnaissance missions.

The Hypersonic SR-72.
(Courtesy Wikipedia)

Lockheed Martin is currently developing the next generation of high-altitude planes, called the SR-72 which could be operational by 2030. This is an unmanned, hypersonic plane capable of flying at Mach 6, or six times the speed of sound, and possibly incorporating a strike platform capable of firing hypersonic missiles. According to Brad Leland at Lockheed-Martin, speed is the next aviation advancement to counter emerging threats. Perhaps this will be the next chapter in our continued journey into reconnaissance.

The introduction phrase used in the 1966 television series, *Star Trek*, began "space, the final frontier." What was then considered a somewhat fictional perception, has become a reality. Space has evolved into an important part of the world economy with many civilian and military systems, such as the Global Positioning System operated by the 50th Space Wing, Schriever AFB, Colorado, dependent on satellites. The Pentagon considers US focus on space an increasing challenge because China and Russia are developing the technological ability to render US satellites non-functional. US military services have discussed the possibility to deploy permanent space sensors to more quickly identify any potential enemy threat to our satellite systems.

The need for concentrating on space has never been greater. Space is considered the strategic location where future conflicts and wars will develop. The most significant US competitor for the control of space is Communist China, which is fully engaged in building space control capabilities. It has developed a space strategy which appears to be on a much more aggressive time line than the US strategy. If unchecked, China may have the ability to shut down America's computer systems, disable and, or, control the power grid, consequently disabling the US military effectiveness worldwide.

In addition to the Air Force and CIA aerial surveillance programs existing today, there is no doubt about the need to continue to improve space surveillance programs. On 21 December 2019, President Donald Trump signed the 2020 National Defense Authorization Act creating the sixth independent military service branch, the Space Force, with the primary mission to maintain US space dominance. Proclaiming space as an expanding national security threat, President Trump stated, "Space is the world's new war-fighting domain. Because of the grave threats to our national security, American superiority in space is absolutely vital," and part of that effort certainly involves an expansion of aerial reconnaissance. The Secretary of State, Mark Espy, stated, "the next big fight may very well start in space, and the US military must be ready." If history does repeat itself, looking back at the truth in General Billy Mitchell's 1918 proclamation that first battles of any future war will be air battles, it behooves the US to consider the first battles in space as a coming reality.

With the increased volatility in space comes the importance to increase our capability for overhead espionage in managing space activities. The Cold War overhead espionage spy planes served their very important purpose in meeting America's challenges to remain a free nation, and will continue to be recognized for the many contributions made to our national defense. Through the work of many dedicated people within these programs, they helped to define and shape our national security policies and decision-making processes far into the future. In this technology driven era, nothing may have the service life of the U-2 or the SR-71 Blackbird, but in the next twenty, or thirty, years, who knows what our capabilities will be, or our need for overhead espionage.

RESOURCE MATERIAL

BOOKS

Anderson, Elizabeth, *Ten strange and obscure incidents from the cold war, June* 15, 2015

Bacevich, Andrew J., *Breach of Trust*, Metropolitan Books, 2013

Baier, Bret, *Three Days in Moscow,* Harper-Collins, *2018*

Berkowitz, Bruce Dr., *the National reconnaissance office at 50 Years: A Brief History,* Center for the Study of National Reconnaissance, 2011

Crickmore, Paul F. *Lockheed SR-71A Blackbird.* Osprey Publishing Ltd., 2015

Graham, Richard H., *Flying the Blackbird*, Zenith Press, 2008

Graham, Richard H., *SR-71A Revealed the Inside Story,* MBI Publishing, 1996

Jane's Encyclopedia of Aviation, *U-2 information*, Crescent Books, 1993

Joiner, Stephen, *RF-4 Operating Information,* 2015, Air Magazine

Michaelson, Steven W. *Sun Tzu for Execution*, Adams Business Publisher, 2007

Murphy, James D., *Business is Combat*, Regan Books, 2000

Murphy, James D., *Flawless Execution*, Harper Collins, 2005

Patterson, Dan, & Dick, Ron, *War and Peace in the Air*, Boston Mills, 2006

Powers, Francis Gary, *Operation Overflight-A memoir of the U-2 Incident,* Potomac Books, 2004

Richardson, Doug, *Combat Arms-Modern Spy Planes,* Prentice Hall Press,1990

Rich, Ben, *Clarence Leonard Kelly Johnson, a Biographical Memoir,* National Academies Press, 1995

The KC-135 Refueling Tanker, *The Vital Guide to Military Aircraft*, Air life Publishing Ltd., 1994

Westad, Odd Arne, *the Cold War-A World History*, Basic Books, subsidiary of Hachette Book Group

NEWSPAPERS AND MAGAZINES

Blitz, Matt, How Civil War Balloonist Changed History, *Popular Mechanics*, May 2017

Cartrette, Nicole, Col. Walter L. Watson, *South Carolina News*, February, 2015

Feature Article, Legend of The Habu, *Combat Aircraft*, April, 2018

Handwerk, Brian, How Area 51 Hid Secret Craft, *National Geographic News* May, 2011

Hennigan, J.W., Inside the new American way of war, *Time Magazine*, December 2017

Isachenkov, Vladimir, Associated Press, *Times Daily*, December 25, 2019

Majors, Bill, Sen. John Glenn's senate speech, *Chicago Tribune*, November,1990

Oliver, Mynra, Kelly Johnson, design pioneer of Lockheed aircraft dies, *Los Angeles Times*, December, 1990, Articles.latimes.com

The Smithsonian Institution, At the Controls, Cataloging-in-publishing Data, 2006

Wince-Smith, Deborah. Global Security, Economic Strength, *American Legion Magazine*, March, 2017

ENCYCLOPEDIAS

The Encyclopedia Britannica, Taylor, John & Guilmartin, John. 2011, "Military Aircraft"

Wikipedia, the free Encyclopedia

DOCUMENTARY FILMS

Blackbird Stealth, *The story of the SR-71A*, 2017, Military History Channel

Spy Planes, *Secret, superpowered Aircraft*, June 2018, The History Channel

QUOTES

Churchill, Winston, Prime Minister, www.brainyquote.com/quotes
Fritsch, Werner von, German General, Military History Now, 2019
Harris, Carlyle S, *Col. Tap Code,* Zondervan Publishers, 2019
Johnson, Kelly, SR-71A Blackbirds, Haynes, Leland R. 1996 www.wvi.com
McCrary, Rick, pilot, SBNATION. Spencer Hall.www.sbnation.com
Wadkins, Jim, Col., Lockheed-Martin, www.lockheedmartin.com

GOVERNMENT INTERNET SITES

A-12 Oxcart, CIA website, Nov 21, 2012, www.cia.gov
Area 51, U-2 and the Accidental Test Flight, CIA News & Information, 2015, www.cia.gov
Gibbs, Yvonne, NASA Armstrong Fact Sheet:SR-71A Blackbird, August 7, 2017, wwwnasa.gov
Historical Document, Lockheed's Aviation Genius, 10/1 2007, www.cia.gov
Majumdar, Dave, Defense Editor, SR-71A Operational Cost Estimates, December 2015, The National Interest Website, www.national interest.org
NASA Dryden Flight Research Center, Edwards AFB, California. SR-71A Statistical data, www.nasa.gov
Reinert, Bob, Natick tube foods keep U-2 pilots flying high, USAG-Natick Public Affairs, January 2013,   www.army.mil
The Office of Technology and Scientific Research (declassified), *Governmentattic.org*
53rd Weather Reconnaissance Squadron, www.403wg.afrc.af.mil

PUBLIC INTERNET SITES

Allison, David, "Personnel who flew the blackbirds." SR-71ABlackbird website, 2004, www.wvi.com
Belenko, Victor, MiG-25, *The Daily Beast*, September, 2017 wwwthedailybeast.com
Dowling, Stephen, "SR-71A Blackbird, The Cold War's Ultimate Spy Plane," BBC.com, July 2013
Garrison, Peter, "Head Skunk", Air & Space Magazine, March 2010, www.airspace.com

Haynes, Leland R., "Habu Information," USAF SR-71A Kadena Operations, February 2005, www.wvi.com

Haynes, Leland R., "SR-71A Fact Sheet," SR-71A Blackbirds, 2004, www.wvi.com

History, "Gorbachev resigns as president of the USSR", www.history.com

Johnson, Kelly, Engineer, www.revolvy.com

Keller, Jarred, "The CIA Had A Top-Secret Manual," task and purpose.com October, 2018

Kucher, Paul R, "Blackbird Records," SR-71A On line, October 2011, www.SR-71A.org

Larson, George C, "John Glenn's Project Bullet," www.airspacemag.com, July 2009

Larsen, Klaus, "When His SR-71A Disintegrated..." (Bill Weaver's crash), www.chuck yeager.org

Lockett, Brian, "Blackbird heat buildup," Air and Space Museum, www.airandspace.com

Miller, Aaron, "29 Facts you didn't know about the SR-71A Blackbird," January 2016. www.thrilllist.com

Murray, Frank, "How They Got There," wwwroadrunnersinternationale.com, April 2015

Prior, Mark, "Oswald and the U-2 program: A Second Look and Yet Another Fascinating Coincidence," Kennedys and King.com, 2012

Reynolds, Linda KC., "Eagles gather in Lancaster for Annual Gathering," October 2015, www.aerotecknews

Roop, Lee, SR-71A News Article, www.al.com/news/Huntsville, 2016

Spacy, William L. Col. USAF (Ret), Air Refueling Archive, airrefuelingarchive.wordpress.com

USAF /Hill ABF, "Flight suit information," www.hill.af.mil, augmented by, "A day in the life of a PSD Technician, Svetocs, Kevin, PSD Instructor, Beale AFB, California, www.wvi.com, March 2004

Document Credits

CIA Manual for Physical Maintenance Control
CIA Memo Oxcart and SR-71A Operation Plan
CIA SR-71A Phase-in Option "A"
Air Combat Command, Physiological Support Equipment Manual for Pilot and RSO Survival Kit Contents

Declassified SR-71A Flight Manual Documents from the Paul R. Kucher SR-71A On Line website.

Section II-figure 2-3 Personal equipment hook up
Section II-figure 2-55 Refueling boom limits
Section I-figure 1-32 Fuel tanks and quantity
Section II-figure 2-67 Landing pattern-typical

Photo Credits

Cover courtesy of the USAAF (public domain photo)
Book photos; CIA, NASA, US Air Force, Hill AFB, Beale AFB, Department of Defense, Dryden Flight Research Center, and Wikimedia Commons. Other photos in this book were taken by employees of these agencies and are in the public domain. A special thanks is extended to: Brian Lockett-Air and Space.com, Paul R. Kucher-SR-71A OnLine, Lt. Col. Dave Fruehauf, and Mike Jetzer/heroicrelics.org for granting permission to use their private photos.

Acknowledgements

A significant part of this book is derived from personal interviews with military service members involved with the Cold War spy plane programs. I am very appreciative to the individuals listed below for their patience, cooperation, and contributions. Each person provided information specific to his/her personal experience and therefore, their endorsement of all information in this book is neither stated, or implied.

Personal Interviews

Lola Wilson Fossett
USAF Staff Sergeant, (Ret) Physiological Support Division Technician
9th Strategic Reconnaissance Wing, Beale AFB, California

David "Dave" E. Fruehauf
USAF Lieutenant Colonel, (Ret) SR-71 Blackbird Pilot 1967-1977

OMS Squadron Commander and OL-8 Detachment Commander
Okinawa, Japan

Preston E. Hillis
USAF Staff Sergeant, Aircraft Loadmaster C-133/ C130
Military Air Transport Service
Dover AFB, Delaware

James Greg Kimbrough
USAF Major, (Ret) U-2 Pilot 2000-2009
War in Afghanistan-Operation Enduring Freedom
9th Strategic Reconnaissance Wing, Beale AFB, California

Roy Price
USAF Staff Sergeant, 100th Security Police Squadron
RAF Mildenhall, Suffolk, England 1983-1992

L. Mark Taylor
USAF Technical Sergeant, (Ret) RF4-C Weapons Specialist
117th Tactical Reconnaissance Wing
Alabama Air National Guard

Raymond Edward "Ed" Yeilding
USAF Lieutenant Colonel, (Ret) SR-71 Blackbird Pilot 1983-1990
SR-71 Pilot Instructor and Developmental Test Pilot
9th Strategic Reconnaissance Wing, Beale AFB, California

CONTRIBUTORS, READERS, AND EDITORS

I also express my gratitude and profound appreciation to the individuals listed below who not only provided information, but spent their valuable time reading and editing all, or part, of the book. It is a better read because of their efforts.

James Franklin
Chief Engineer, Special Projects Office (Ret)
Marshall Space Flight Center, Huntsville, Alabama

Gary M. Green
Professor of Geography, University of North Alabama (Ret)
US Army Specialist 4, Cartographer

Francis Gary Powers Jr.
Founder & Chairman Emeritus, the Cold War Museum, Fairfax, VA

Eizens Paul Silins
US Army Artillery and Ordnance Disposal Officer (Ret)

Albert "Al" Virden,
USAF Senior Master Sergeant, Communications Specialist (Ret)
Osan Air Base, Korea

ABOUT THE AUTHOR

Charles E Cabler is a six-year (1962–1968) USAF veteran serving at the 3800 Air Base Wing, Maxwell AFB, Montgomery, Alabama; the 1094 Support Squadron Manzano Base, Albuquerque, New Mexico; and the Air Force Reserve, Denver, Colorado. Charles served during the Cuban Missile Crisis and the Vietnam War, earning the National Defense Medal with Ribbon, and service award ribbons for longevity, and training, and certificates for small arms expert marksmanship. He is a member of the American Legion, Post 11 in Florence, Alabama, and a volunteer adviser for the American Corporate Partners Organization providing career guidance to military personnel as they transition into civilian life.

Charles retired after a forty-three-year career in the financial services industry with AmSouth, First Union, Wachovia and Wells Fargo banks. He is a graduate of the Alabama School of Banking at the University of South Alabama. He served as a faculty member for the banking industry's training schools at the University of Oklahoma, Indiana University-Purdue University at Indianapolis (IUPUI), the Alabama Regulatory Compliance Institute, and was the Director of the Wachovia Lending Compliance School. As a Subject Matter Expert, he was an instructor in continuing education programs for the Chicago, San Francisco and Dallas Federal Reserve Banks. He is a volunteer teacher for two Florence High School Career Development Education programs, Launch* and 12 For Life*, helping students acquire a better understanding of the business environment prior to graduating. He is a member of the USAF Police Alumni Association, the Shoals Writers Guild, the Tennessee Valley Historical Society.

He has authored the following books available through Amazon.com: *What Every Employee Should Know To Be Successful, Elements To Consider As A First Time Manager, Creating A Competitive Advantage*, and *The Chains of Marley.*

CPSIA information can be obtained
at www.ICGtesting.com
Printed in the USA
LVHW081728140721
692519LV00002BA/18